WITHDRAWN

Cambridge Topics in Geography Series
Editors: F.C. Evans and M.A. Morgan

RURAL AFRICA

Already published in this series:
Hugh Clout: *The regional problem in western Europe*
Andrew Goudie and John Wilkinson: *The warm desert environment*
Roger Robinson: *Ways to move: the geography of networks and accessibility*
David Ingle Smith and Peter Stopp: *The river basin: an introduction to the study of hydrology*

A.T. Grove & F.M.G. Klein

RURAL AFRICA

CAMBRIDGE UNIVERSITY PRESS
Cambridge
London   New York   Melbourne

Published by the Syndics of the Cambridge University Press
The Pitt Building, Trumpington Street, Cambridge CB2 1RP
Bentley House, 200 Euston Road, London NW1 2DB
32 East 57th Street, New York, NY 10022, USA
296 Beaconsfield Parade, Middle Park, Melbourne 3206, Australia

© Cambridge University Press 1979

First published 1979

Printed in Great Britain at the University Press, Cambridge

Library of Congress Cataloguing in Publication Data
Grove, Alfred Thomas.
Rural Africa.
(Cambridge topics in geography series)
Bibliography: p.
1. Africa — Description and travel — 1977 —
2. Anthropo-geography — Africa. I. Klein, Frances, joint author. II. Title.
DT12.25.G76   333.7'6'096   77-82496
ISBN 0 521 21825 X hard covers
ISBN 0 521 29282 4 paperback

CONTENTS

Introduction   1

1 Ecological systems   5
   Climates and ecosystems   5

2 Human systems   15
   Agricultural systems   16
   Ethnic differentiation   22
   Subsistence agriculture   23
   Commercial agriculture   27
   National differentiation   28

3 The humid forest lands   31
   Hunting and gathering   33
   Cultivation   34
   Timber   42
   Cocoa in Ghana   42
   Plantations in Cameroun   45

4 The savanna lands   48
   Hunters   50
   Burning vegetation   50
   Pastoralism   51
   Cultivation   54
   Modernisation of farming   64

5 The arid lands   69
   The Bushmen   70
   Pastoralism   71
   Somali transhumance   72
   Pastoralism in the Sudan Republic   74
   Irrigation   75

6 Mountain, river, lake and coastal lands   81
   Mountains   81
   Riverine areas   88
   Lakes and their shores   92
   Coastal areas   96

7 Movement and communications   99
   Transport and trade routes   99
   Markets and marketing   108
   Trading   111
   Religion   113
   Services   114
   Movements of people   117

Conclusion   119

Further reading list   120

Index   121

ACKNOWLEDGEMENTS

Thanks are due to the following for permission to reproduce figures and tables or other original material. The number in brackets is the figure or table number.

Figures. [1] C.R.W. Spedding, *The Biology of Agricultural Systems*, Academic Press, London, 1975. [4] B.W. Hodder and D.R. Harris, *Africa in Transition*, Methuen, 1967. [12, 18] A.N. Duckham and G.B. Masefield, *Farming Systems of the World*, Chatto and Windus, 1970. [14, 17, 27] W.B. Morgan, in M.F. Thomas and G.W. Whittington, *Environment and Land Use in Africa*, Methuen, 1969. [15 G.P. Murdock,] *Africa*, McGraw-Hill, USA, 1959. [21] R.T. Jackson, in *East African Geographical Review*, 1970. [23] R.J. Horvath, in *Annals of the Association of American Geographers*, **59**, 1969. [24] A.I. Richards, F. Sturrock and J.M. Fortt, eds., *Subsistence to Commercial Farming in Present-Day Buganda*, Cambridge, 1973. [29] R. Dumont, *Types of Rural Economy*, Methuen, 1957. [32] W.B. Morgan and J.C. Pugh, *West Africa*, Barnes and Noble, USA; Methuen, 1969. [33] H.A. Oluwasanmi, *Uboma* (Occasional Paper 6), Geographical Publications, 1966. [34] B. Floyd, *Eastern Nigeria*, Macmillan, 1969. [37] P. Hill, *Migrant Cocoa-Farmers of Southern Ghana*, Cambridge, 1963. [38] C. Okali and R.A. Kotey, *Akokoaso* (Technical Publication Series 15), ISSER, University of Ghana, 1971. [43, 44] D.J. Stenning, *Savanna Nomads*, International African Institute, 1959. [45] A.R. James. [46, 47] A.I. Richards, *Land Labour and Diet in Northern Rhodesia*, International African Institute, 1939. [49, 93] P. and L. Bohannan, *Tiv Economy*, Northwestern University Press, Evanston, Ill., 1968. [50, 51, 52] D. Rotenhan, in H. Ruthenberg, *Smallholder Farming and Smallholder Development in Tanzania*, Ifo-Institut, Munich, 1968. [53, 55] M.J. Mortimore and J. Wilson, *Land and People in the Kano Close Settled Zone*, Department of Geography, Ahmadu Bello University, Nigeria, 1965. [57, 58] D.R.F. Taylor, in M.F. Thomas and G.W. Whittington, *Environment and Land Use in Africa*, Methuen, 1969. [61] R.B. Lee, in R.L. Smith, *The Ecology of Man*, Harper and Row, NY, 1972. [62] R.B. Lee and I. Devore, *Man the Hunter*, Aldine Publishing Company, Chicago, 1968. [63] R.M. Prothero, *Migrants and Malaria*, Longmans, 1965. [64] H.R.J. Davies, in *Tijdschrift voor Economische en Sociale Geographie*, 1966. [65] J.H.G. Lebon, *Land Use in Sudan*, Geographical Publications, 1965. [69] J.C. de Wilde, *Experiences with Agricultural Development in Tropical Africa 2*, The Johns Hopkins Press, Baltimore, Md., 1967. [71] H. Smeds, in *Acta Geographica*, 1955. [72, 73] J.-C. Froelich, *Les Montagnards "Paleonigritiques"*, Editions Berger Levrault, 1968. [79] P.J. Wagland, in *Geography*, 1969. [82] I. Wilks, *Asante in the Nineteenth Century*, Cambridge, 1975. [83] A. Mabogunje, *Urbanisation in Nigeria*, Africana Publishing Company, a Division of Holmes and Meier, USA; University of London, 1968. [88] E.J. Taaffe, R. Morrill and P. Gould, in *Geographical Review*, 1963. [89] B. Hoyle, in R.H. Osborne, F.A. Barnes and J.C. Doornkamp, *Geographical Essays in Honour of K.C. Edwards*, Department of Geography, University of Nottingham, 1970. [91, 91] R.H.T. Smith, in T. Meillassoux, *The Development of Indigenous Trade and Markets in West Africa*, Oxford, 1971. [96] F.J. Pedler, *Economic Geography of West Africa*, Longmans, 1955. [99] J. Riddel, *Spatial Dynamics of Modernisation in Sierra Leone*, Northwestern University Press, Evanston, Ill., 1970.

Tables. [1] J. Tricart, *The Landforms of the Humid Tropics*, St Martin's Press, NY; Longmans, 1972. [2] H. Lieth and R.H. Whittaker, *Primary Productivity of the Biosphere*, Springer Verlag, NY, 1975. [6] P. and L. Bohannan, *Tiv Economy*, Northwestern University Press, Evanston, Ill., 1968. [7] H.D. Ludwig, in H. Ruthenberg, *Smallholder Farming and Smallholder Development in Tanzania*, Ifo-Institut, Munich, 1968. [15] A. Mabogunje, *Urbanisation in Nigeria*, Africana Publishing Company, a Division of Holmes and Meier, USA; University of London, 1968. [20] F. Wilson, *Labour in the South African Gold Mines, 1911–1969*, Cambridge, 1972.

Photographs. [26, 35, 41, 49] African Studies Centre, University of Cambridge. [28, 60] A.T. Grove. [40] Institut Geographique National, Paris. [30, 54, 75, 90] Fergus Wilson.

Drawings are by Reg Piggott.

INTRODUCTION

In this volume we illustrate some of the relationships which exist between man and the land in tropical Africa. We consider three major ecological zones and four more specialised environments. The most significant factor underlying the differences between the ecological zones is the variation in climate, particularly the amount and distribution of rainfall. Each zone has specific characteristics which are expressed in the natural vegetation. The forest is an area where plant growth takes place almost continuously throughout the year; the savanna experiences seasonal growth associated with the seasonal availability of moisture, and the desert 'flowers' briefly and sporadically when local conditions are favourable. These varying environmental conditions pose diverse problems for the inhabitants.

Viewed as an element in the natural world, man can occupy land in three main ways. He can remain part of the natural order, gathering wild produce and hunting for animals. At any one time he obtains only his immediate requirements, principally food, since material possessions hardly exist. A small number of people range over a wide area of land but, given adequate territory, sufficient food supplies can be found and life is not particularly strenuous. Contacts with other groups of people are very limited and there is little need for links with an external economic order. The areas open to hunters and gatherers have been greatly reduced over the years as other economic activities encroach on their territories. There are now only a few such groups in existence in tropical Africa and these have been pushed into areas which are unattractive economically.

More commonly in tropical Africa, man occupies the land as a subsistence producer. He endeavours to control limited sections of his environment in order to produce specific kinds of food. In many instances he tries to simulate the diversity he sees in nature both in the crops he grows and the methods he uses. By herding animals or cultivating crops, larger numbers of people can live in smaller areas than would be required for successful hunting and gathering. Subsistence occupancy destroys the natural equilibrium but, given sufficient land and ingenuity, a fragile balance is achieved. Three main forms of subsistence production are illustrated in this volume: shifting cultivation, rotational fallow cultivation and permanent cultivation. The system used by any one group of people depends on many factors, in particular the local population density and the natural fertility of the land. In some areas, the pressure of population is such that the fragile balance is crumbling and the natural fertility is being lost. Subsistence producers are to a large extent self reliant but they do have links with adjacent groups and state authorities.

1 The countries of Africa

The third kind of man's occupancy of the land is that of commercial exploitation. The produce is generally exported outside tropical Africa, while energy and other essential inputs such as fertilisers and machinery are at present imported from non-African countries. Ecological considerations, except for the broad requirements needed for optimum growth of specific crops, are less important than economic and political realities, such as world prices and government policies. With careful management commercial agriculture is not destructive of fertility. This, after all, is a basic asset of the commercial farmers, but the potential for destruction is great if compensatory inputs and techniques are omitted. Commercial agriculture is part of the world economic system and has links with local, national and international organisations.

Cross-cutting these three broad forms of occupancy in Africa are patterns of social and political organisation. Ethnic groupings are a basic feature of rural African life. Specific ethnic groups are frequently associated with particular forms of land use. Many responses to environmental conditions and to changes in life styles or work procedures are influenced by the ideas and values of the different communities. The variety of agricultural systems found in the second form of occupancy, primarily subsistence — with which much of this book is concerned — are the result of these evaluations. Contact between Africa and the rest of the world through trade, colonial rule, state formation and the experiences of the independent countries has added another organisational framework and other sets of values. State boundaries cut across ethnic areas, for instance that of the Ewe, who live on both sides of the Ghana-Togo border, or traditional grazing grounds on the Somali-Ethiopian border (Fig. 1).

The settlement of Europeans particularly in east and central Africa has both stimulated the commercial development of the areas and created problems of land distribution and political control which are still in the process of being resolved. The trade patterns developed in the colonial era, in which African primary produce is sold to pay for the import of manufactured goods, still dominate the trade of African countries. Attempts are being made to change this but progress is slow. Mainline communications in most African states are aligned to the needs of the export trade and links with overseas countries rather than movement within and between neighbouring states. The development of air travel has led to a greater amount of movement between African states, but this rarely affects the rural dweller significantly since his very small income does not permit him the luxury of inter-state or overseas travel.

The rate of population growth in Africa is higher than that of any other continent. Although tropical Africa at present has a very small percentage of its population living in towns, people are rapidly moving into urban areas. With an increasing population and a growing urban population there is a dual need for food production to be expanded. In the past, the stress placed on export crops meant that little attention was given to improving local food supplies or domestic marketing organisations. More emphasis is now being placed on policies aimed at stimulating food production; for instance, Ghana has 'Operation Feed Yourself' and Nigeria 'Operation Feed the Nation'. The increase of the commercial element in subsistence farming, however, must be achieved without the destruction of the fragile ecological balance. The ramifications of increasing production are numerous, including the development of credit and loan facilities, technical education, road construction, and distribution and marketing organisations. Such developments could go some way to evening up the pattern of development in Africa which at the moment is very much one of 'islands of development'. One of the great problems is that even where productivity has increased substantially in some export commodities, the value of the produce to the producer and the state has declined because of low world prices, currency fluctuations and inflation. The rising price of oil has had severe effects on the budgets of most tropical African states, and particularly on poor countries like Tanzania which have few commodities for export.

Compared with Europe, North America and Japan, rural tropical Africa is an area characterised by its general poverty. Three of the four states at the bottom of the World Bank's table of gross national products per capita in 1975 are African countries: Mali, Upper Volta and Rwanda. The economic gap between the rich and poor countries of the world is widening and ways must be found of closing it.

1

Ecological systems

Two-thirds of the people of tropical Africa live on the land and spend a large proportion of their time producing food. Compared with Europe or North America, towns are few and employment in industry is very limited. This book considers the rural environment and the life of the majority of the population.

The term 'rural tropical Africa' describes most of the land area in Africa between the tropics of Cancer and Capricorn. It is an area of diversity of physical backgrounds, ethnic groupings, languages, cultures, economic and social systems, and political ideologies and regimes. In a short study of this kind it is necessary to be selective and concentrate on certain features. As agriculture, in one form or other, dominates the lives of rural Africans it is this that is taken as the main theme. Agriculture involves man working with the natural environment to exploit living or biological processes in order to produce goods, usually food, but also raw materials for manufacturing industries (Fig. 2). We therefore intend to begin this study by looking at the living processes within the natural environment of tropical Africa.

Climates and ecosystems

In the natural environment sunlight and heat, soil, water, vegetation and wildlife are all related to each other in such a way that a change in any one would cause changes in the others. The natural environment is an inter-related system and sunlight and heat, water, soil, vegetation and wildlife are components of this system. Within the overall global system there are numerous sub-groups called ecosystems which can be studied either within the context of the overall system or on their own. Any particular ecosystem consists of a collection of plants, animals and non-living substances which are inter-acting with one another. It need be no larger than a small rock pool but it can be an entire forest. Each ecosystem contains four components: the non-living substances (air, water and rock), the

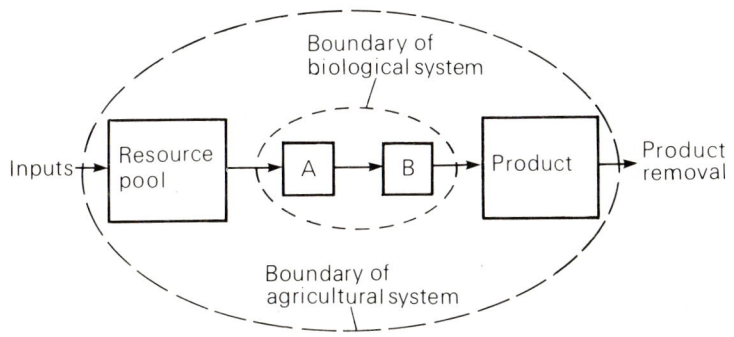

2 The simplest possible representation of the way in which a biological system with only two components A and B may operate within an agricultural system converting resources into products. For example, nitrogenous fertiliser might be one input adding to the soil nitrogen pool, used by grass (A), subsequently eaten by cows (B) producing milk

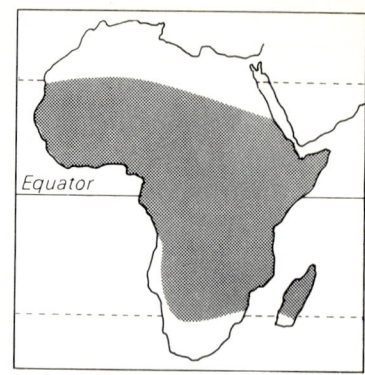

3 The area of Africa where the average daily range of temperature exceeds the average annual range

producers (green plants), the consumers (grazing animals), and the decomposers (bacteria and fungi) which break down organic matter and release substances the producers can use. All these components should interact in such a way that there is a balance between consumption, growth and decomposition, creating and maintaining a condition of stability or equilibrium. If one or other of the components gets out of balance it may drastically change the system. For example, if the number of animals grazing an area is excessive the animals may destroy the vegetation completely; on the other hand if large grazing animals are kept out of an area it may be overrun by ferns in highland areas or thorny bushes on semi-arid plains. For the purpose of this study we will concentrate on three sets of ecosystems — called ecological zones — found in tropical Africa and consider in a further chapter four special ecosystems associated with areas where the influence of topography or surface water is particularly great. The main reason for the differences between these ecological zones is the variation in climate over tropical Africa, in particular the amount and distribution of precipitation.

Temperature

Mean annual temperatures in tropical Africa exceed 20 °C, except at high altitudes, and seasonal variations in temperature are small (Table 1). Indeed in most of tropical Africa the average daily range of temperature exceeds the average annual range of temperature (Fig. 3). There are, however, differences in temperature between the eastern and western parts of the continent; the west generally lies below 1000 metres (m), but most of the east is well above that altitude. Mean annual temperatures diminish by about 1 °C for every 150 m increase in height. Throughout the year tropical areas experience a day length of approximately twelve hours. It is the differences in humidity and rainfall which are responsible for the profound contrasts in vegetation between, for instance, the Sahara Desert and the tropical rain forests of Zaïre.

Table 1. Temperature ranges in tropical Africa

Place	Average temperature of coolest month (°C)	Average temperature of warmest month (°C)	Range
Dakar, Senegal	21.7	28.9	7.2
Kayes, Mali	27.2	35.6	8.4
Bobo-Dioulasso, Upper Volta	25.0	31.1	6.1
Conakry, Guinea	26.1	27.8	1.7
Beyla, Guinea	22.8	25.6	2.8
Abidjan, Ivory Coast	26.1	28.3	2.2
Douala, Cameroun	23.9	26.7	2.8
Entebbe, Uganda	21.0	23.5	2.5
Kinshasa, Zaïre	22.0	27.0	5.0
Tamatave, Malagasy Republic	20.5	26.6	6.1

4 The rains move north and south with the sun, and are associated with the deep moist air on the equatorwards side of the inter-tropical convergence a. Africa's global position in relation to pressure systems and the inter-tropical convergence zone; b. rainfall patterns associated with the frontal systems in January and July; c. section through the inter-tropical convergence zone from the Gulf of Guinea to the Sahara in July

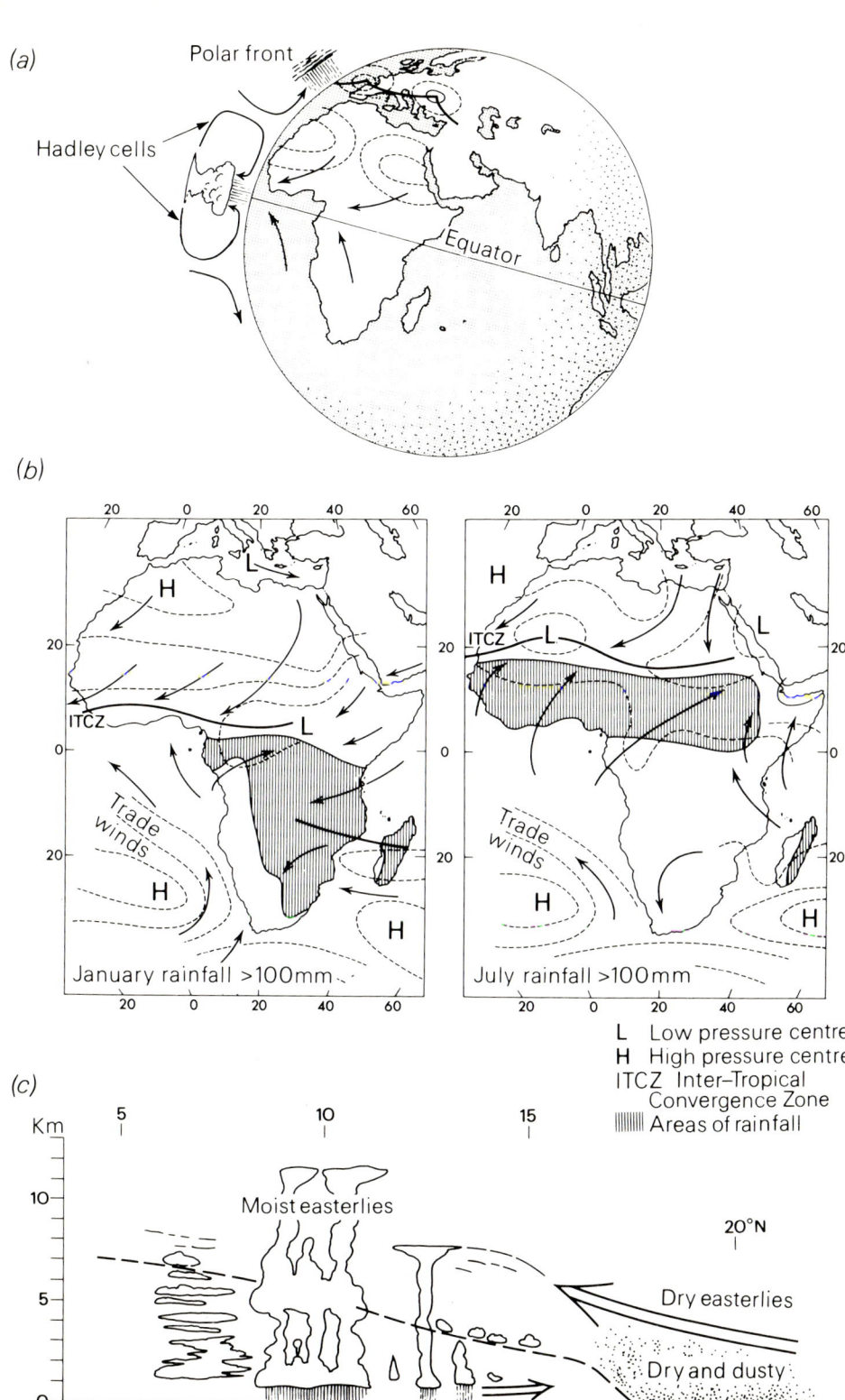

Precipitation and air systems

The pattern of rainfall over the continent is governed largely by the movement of the atmosphere (Fig. 4). There are two great circulatory systems of air which are dominant over inter-tropical Africa; these are called Hadley cells. When the sun is overhead at the equator (the March and September equinoxes), the heated air rises and diverges at a height of a few thousand metres, some air flowing north and some south. There is a strong flow of air towards the equator and this acquires an easterly component because of the earth's rotation. These easterly winds are the trade winds. Since the earth moves round the sun in a slightly elliptical orbit and with its axis tilted at an angle of 66½° to the plane of the orbit, the mid-day sun is overhead 23½° north of the equator in June, at the tropic of Cancer, and 23½° south in December, at the tropic of Capricorn. The Hadley cells move north and south in a manner similar to the apparent movement of the overhead sun but with a lag of a few weeks. Consequently, in the northern hemisphere summer, airstreams blowing across the south Atlantic from south-east to north-west swing round as they cross the equator and approach the Guinea coast of west Africa from the south-west. These moist oceanic air masses undercut the north-easterly air from the interior; the surface between the two air masses slopes gently down from the south towards the north. Although it is sometimes called the Inter-tropical Front, this discontinuity is less well defined than the fronts that are features of depressions in mid-latitudes, and meteorologists often refer to it as the Inter-tropical Convergence Zone or ITCZ. A belt of moist air about 500 km broad follows the movement of the ITCZ, which moves at a rate of about 300 km per month.

The rains begin along the west African coast, the northern part of the Zaïre basin and over Lake Victoria in the early months of the year, and by July have spread to the southern margins of the Sahara and central Ethiopia. At about this time parts of the southern coast of west Africa and larger tracts of land near the equator in east Africa experience a dry season in most years. In September the ITCZ recedes towards the equator more rapidly than it advanced and as the rainfall belt moves south and across the equator the equatorial lands experience another rainfall peak. South of the equator the rains fall mainly between November and March (Fig. 5).

The mean annual rainfall and the length of the rainy season in west Africa diminish from the equator towards the north and, whereas there are two rainy seasons separated by drier seasons near the equator, towards the tropics the rains show one sharply defined annual peak. On the higher eastern side of the continent, the pattern of distribution of the rainfall is more complicated, amounts depending greatly on altitude and exposure. Those parts of Ethiopia, Kenya, Tanzania and Mozambique lying to the east of the rift valley system receive rain from air drawn in from the Indian Ocean, giving highest rainfall values near the coast and at moderate altitudes on the eastern slopes of the highlands. Along the south Atlantic coast dry conditions extend northwards from the Namib Desert into Angola, because the south-easterlies are dry and air approaching from over the ocean is chilled in the lower layers by the cool upwelling waters

5 Mean monthly rainfall and mean monthly temperature at representative places. The temperatures have been plotted in such a way that they represent, crudely, potential evapo-transpiration losses in mm. Where the rainfall bars lie below the temperature line there is a deficit of water; where it rises above there is a surplus

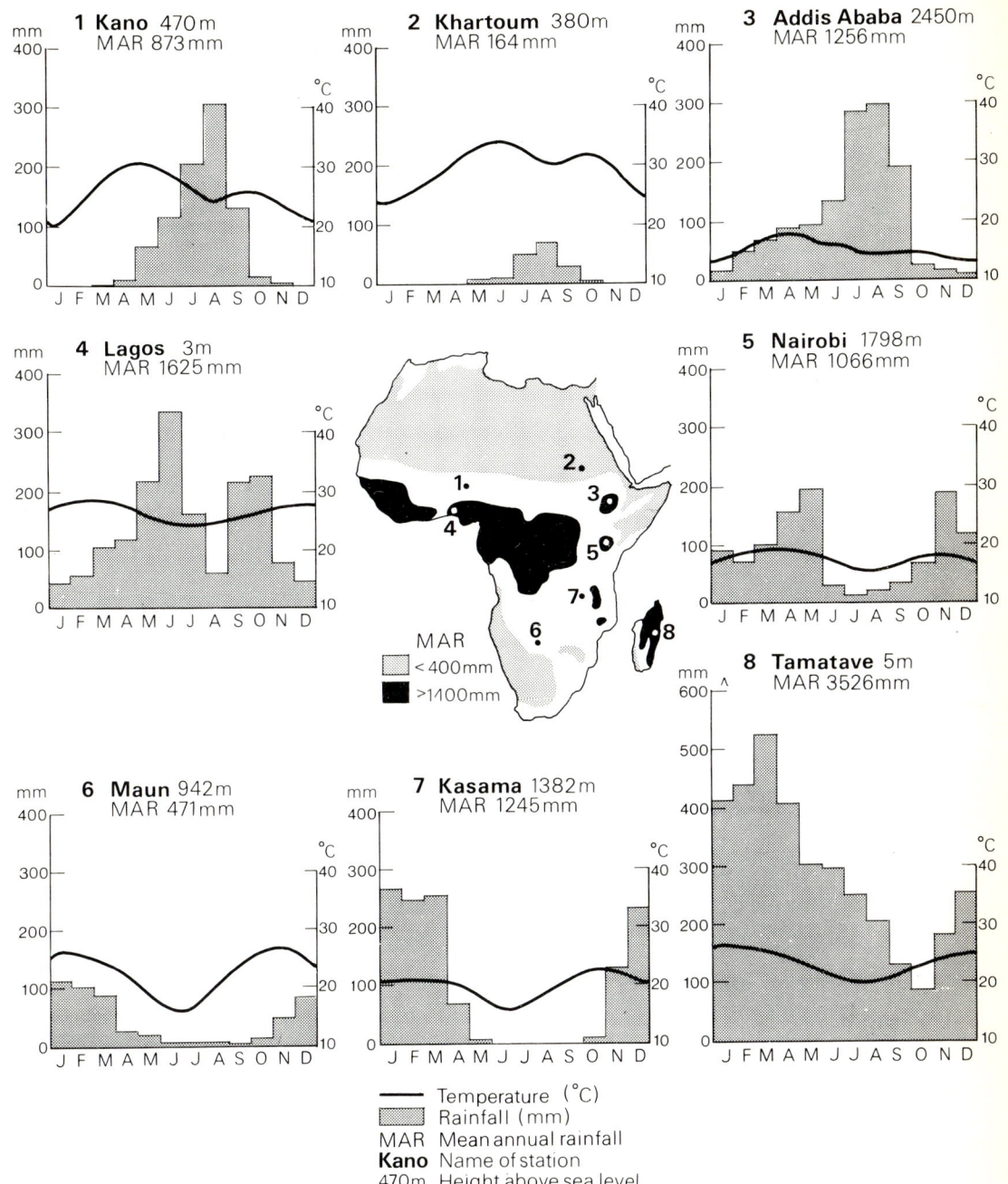

of the Benguela current and is consequently very stable when it comes to pass over the land mass.

The amount and distribution of the rainfall varies not only from season to season but also from year to year and from decade to decade. Exactly why this should be so is not fully understood. A large part of the variability through time is of a random character but there is a tendency for a number of dry years to follow one

6 Rainfall patterns in east Africa

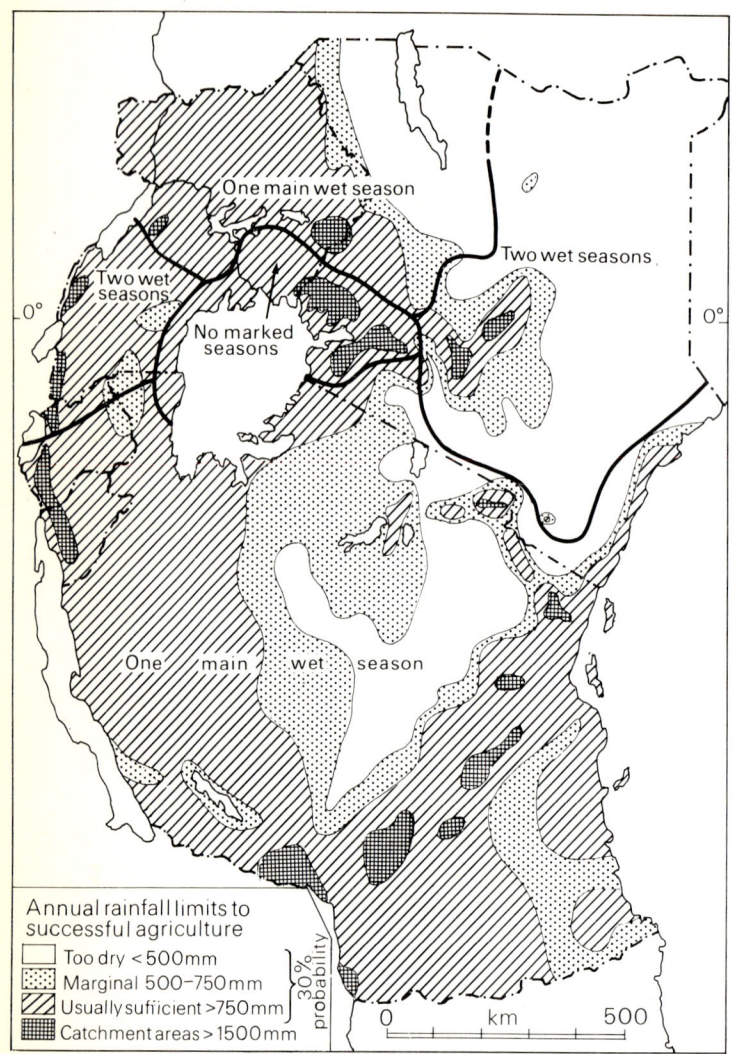

another and for wet years also to be bunched. The variability of rainfall in many areas of tropical Africa is one of the major problems for the farmer. As can be seen in Fig. 6 a large area of east Africa has such unreliable rainfall that successful agriculture is virtually impossible. Much remains to be learned about the causes and distribution of rainfall before long- or short-range weather forecasting can be of much use to the farmer and livestock owner in tropical Africa.

Ecosystems and other systems
The climate largely determines plant productivity. As the temperatures are consistently high throughout the year it is the amount and distribution of water supply which is crucial. Where rainfall is almost continuous during the year, luxuriant vegetation is able to grow throughout the twelve months. Where rainfall is seasonal vegetation is frequently able to grow only during the rainy season. In arid areas where rainfall is sporadic and uncertain, vegetation has either adapted to the dry conditions or grows only when moisture levels

7 Schematic representation of tropical ecosystems and their relationship to the length of the dry season and altitude

are adequate. Each climatic region has its own combination of opportunities and restraints as far as plants and animals are concerned and each has its own specific sets of ecosystems (Fig. 7). We are going to look at the following three large sets of ecosystems (three ecological zones) that are caused by climatic differences, and then a group of four smaller sets of ecosystems that have specific topographical features.

a. Humid lands with mean annual rainfall totals exceeding 1400 mm; these are capable of supporting tropical rain forest.
b. Subhumid lands with rainfall totals between about 400 mm and 1400 mm per annum — enough to support woodland and crop production; these are the savanna lands.
c. Arid lands with less than 400 mm mean annual rainfall, where crop production requires irrigation and pastoralism is dominant.

In addition there are

d. Mountain, river, lake and coastal environments — the four areas where the influence of topography and surface water are particularly great.

In physical geography one can study the movement of water over the earth as a system. The primary energy input is from the sun. Differential heating of the equatorial and polar regions sets up circulatory movements within the atmosphere and the oceans, with heat being transferred polewards by warm air and the latent heat of evaporation of the water vapour the air contains, as well as by warm ocean currents like the Gulf Stream. Cooler air and water move towards the equator, the Benguela current being an instance of the latter. The Hadley cells, mentioned earlier, form a part of the circulatory movement in this great air–ocean system.

The winds blowing over the tropical oceans are the main source of moisture in the atmosphere. When the air is chilled, commonly as a result of upward movement, the water vapour condenses into very small droplets, forming cloud. Continued ascent sets in motion rain-forming processes and the water returns to the oceans or falls on land. There it either evaporates, sinks into the ground or runs into rivers and reaches the sea or evaporates from lakes. The system can

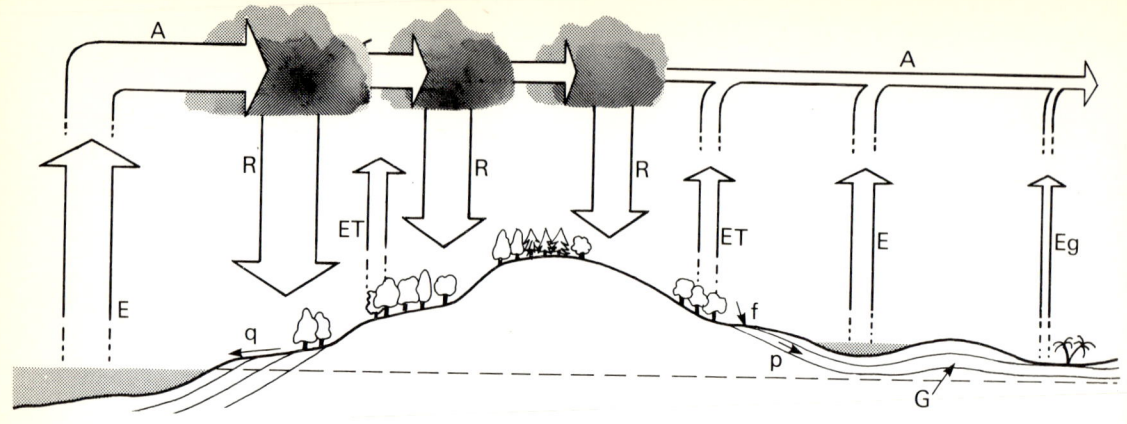

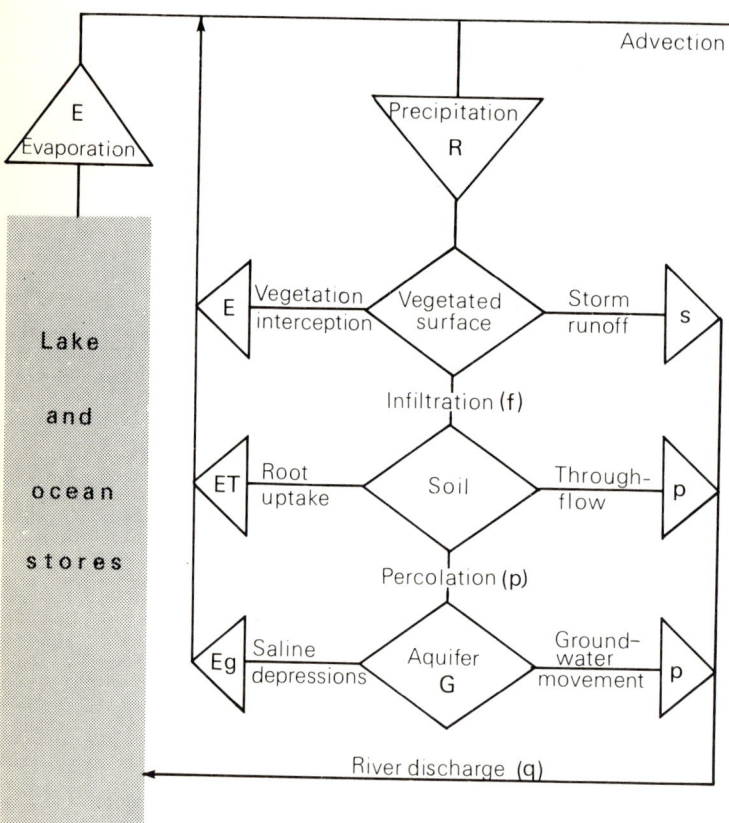

be portrayed as in Fig. 8. Under African conditions, losses of water from the ground by evaporation and by transpiration from the vegetation are everywhere great because of the high temperatures, and these losses (known collectively as evapo-transpiration losses) are potentially greatest in arid lands where skies are clear and the air is dry.

Ecological systems involve not only water and the energy transformations involved in the changes of state from gas to liquid and liquid to solid ice, but also the circulatory systems of the different elements constituting and moving through plants and animals and the soil. As organic substances are formed by living things, solar

8 The hydrographic cycle, in pictorial form (above) and as a systems diagram (below)

9 Energy flow in a simple ecological system

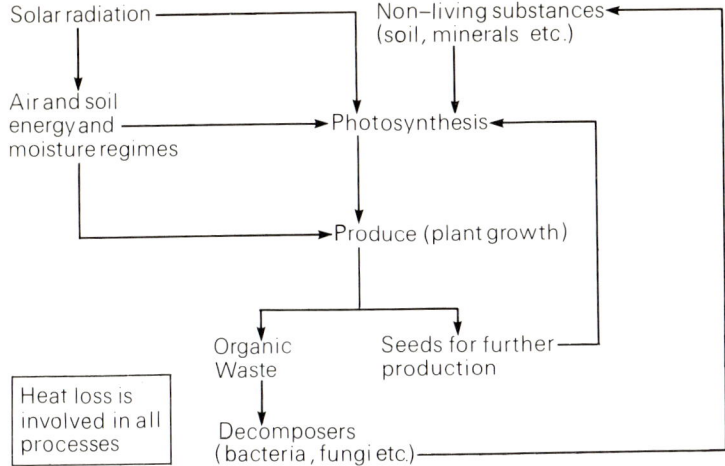

energy is taken up and stored in chemical form, later to be released in the processes of breakdown and decay usually involving oxidation (Fig. 9).

The building-up of organic matter is largely the work of plant leaves. Containing chlorophyll, they utilise light energy from the sun to manufacture plant material, employing carbon dioxide from the atmosphere and hydrogen and other elements from water in the soil. This is the process of photosynthesis; the rate at which it takes place is largely controlled by the amount of sunlight. A good deal of the energy taken up by the plants, however, is released by them again in the form of heat, as they maintain and form new cell material. These losses are called respiration; the rate at which this takes place increases with increasing temperatures in the surrounding air. This can be summarised as follows:

Plant productivity = Photosynthesis — Respiration

In the tropics, even if rainfall is adequate for plant growth and photosynthesis is quite high throughout the year, respiration losses are also high, at any rate at low altitudes, and so plant productivity is limited and not much greater than in middle latitudes.

Some of the plant material synthesised is in the form of leaves and twigs which either fall to the ground and are decomposed or are eaten by insects and other consumers that may in turn be eaten by carnivores. The energy and nutrient substances taken up by the growing plants are released in the processes of breakdown and decomposition of the leaves and other parts, in the faeces of the consumers, and with the death and decay of the consumers and carnivores. Some of the energy and nutrients may accumulate for decades, being stored in the trunks, branches and roots as they grow; but eventually they too die and decompose. Within the forest, savanna and arid ecosystems a host of interacting cycles of energy, water and nutrient substances are in motion.

A single square kilometre of the surface of the earth may receive 2 000 000 kilocalories (8400 MJ) of solar radiation each year. A great deal of this incident radiation is immediately reflected back, especially if the surface is bare as in deserts or severely eroded areas.

Even in the case of rain forest only a very small percentage of the incident radiation is used in gross primary production. Some goes to heat up the forest canopy which itself radiates some back into the atmosphere. The greatest part, in the case of forest vegetation, is utilised in the evaporation of water, such as raindrops on leaves and especially moisture taken up by tree roots from the soil and transpired through the leaves.

At the drier margins of the rain forest and in the savanna nearly all the rain that falls, except in the heaviest storms and at the wettest times of the year, is taken up by tree roots and returned to the atmosphere. Relatively little water is left over to percolate down to feed groundwater and streams. Rivers in the tropics are typically strongly seasonal in their flow: the smaller water-courses are often dry for most of the year; the larger rivers rise during the rainy season and may continue to flow for some weeks into the dry season.

Analyses of water from catchments covered by tropical moist forest usually show that the concentration of dissolved substances in the water is very low indeed, say some 20 parts per million (ppm), which compares with 200 to 500 ppm in much of south-east England. The dissolved substances consist mainly of the bicarbonates, sulphates and chlorides of calcium, potassium, sodium and magnesium, together with silica. Some of these substances, notably the silica, have no doubt been leached from the soil and weathering rock, and their washing out represents a loss from the system. In the savanna lands and semi-arid regions the concentration of dissolved material in the river water is higher, probably because more of the rainwater is lost by evaporation back into the atmosphere. But it has to be borne in mind that the rain itself contains salty substances in solution and they account for a proportion of the dissolved load carried down to the ocean. Under natural conditions the heat and chemical energy leaving an ecosystem over a period of years will equal the solar energy taken in. The nutrients being carried away in river water will be balanced by gains from the atmosphere and the weathering of bedrock. A state of balance or equilibrium exists in such an ecosystem.

At any one time a good deal of energy is stored as chemical energy in the organic matter of the plants, in living creatures and in the soil humus. The amount of dry organic matter stored in living plants and animals is called the biomass and is usually measured in tonnes per sq. km. As a general rule the biomass is likely to vary with the mean annual rainfall (Table 2).

Table 2. Dry-matter production and biomass of ecological zones

Ecological zone	Net primary production in tonnes/hectare/year	Biomass in tonnes/hectare
Tropical rain forest (> 1400 mm)	20	450
Savanna woodland (400–1400 mm)	10	40
Semi-desert scrub (< 400 mm)	1	10

2

Human systems

Man operates within a natural ecological system when he simply collects his food from the environment, just as other animals do (Fig. 10). He gathers sufficient for his needs from week to week and perhaps has a feast when a large animal is killed. Small numbers of people with large areas of land at their disposal, within which they can collect and hunt, live very satisfactorily and enjoy more varied and nutritious diets than some agriculturalists. When numbers increase, however, above a certain low level and the people cease to be merely hunters and collectors, human interference upsets the natural balance (Fig. 11). By clearing and burning the vegetation, grazing their cattle and other beasts, encouraging the growth of a few plants which they find useful and discouraging others they regard as weeds, men reduce the complexity of natural ecosystems. With the prevailing high temperatures in the tropics, destruction of the dominant canopy of vegetation is rapidly followed by the liberation of energy and nutrients locked up in the vegetation and soils. Termites and micro-organisms break down the detritus and organic material; intense rain strikes the soil itself instead of the

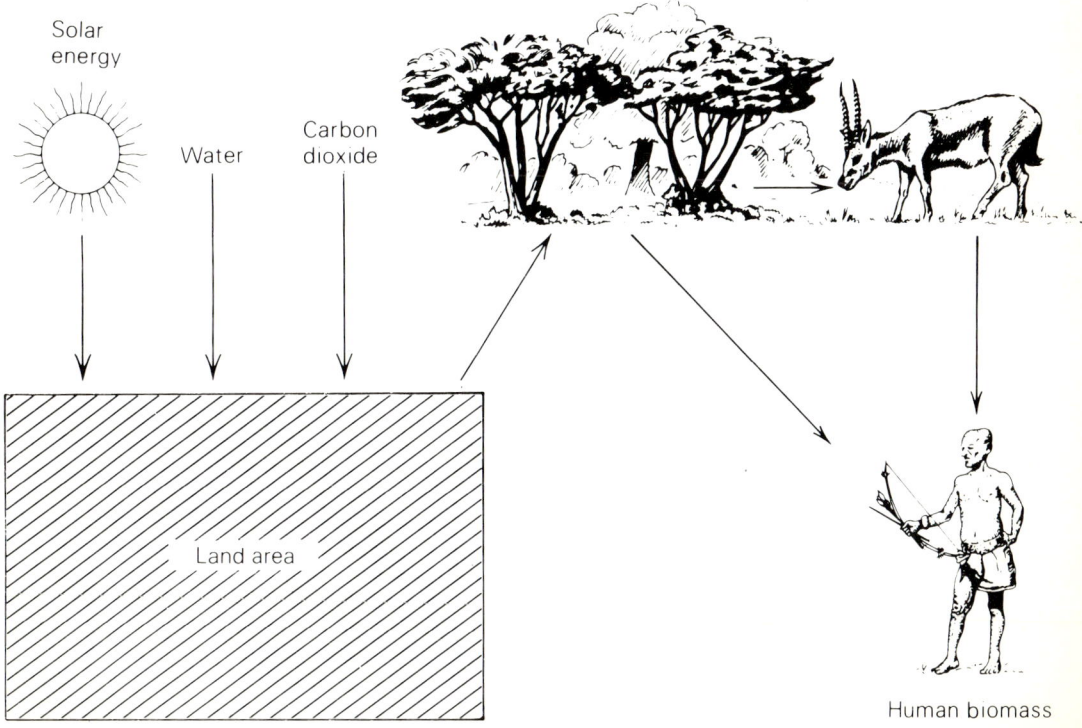

10 The natural ecological system, with man hunting and collecting

11 The effect of man's agriculture on the ecological cycle

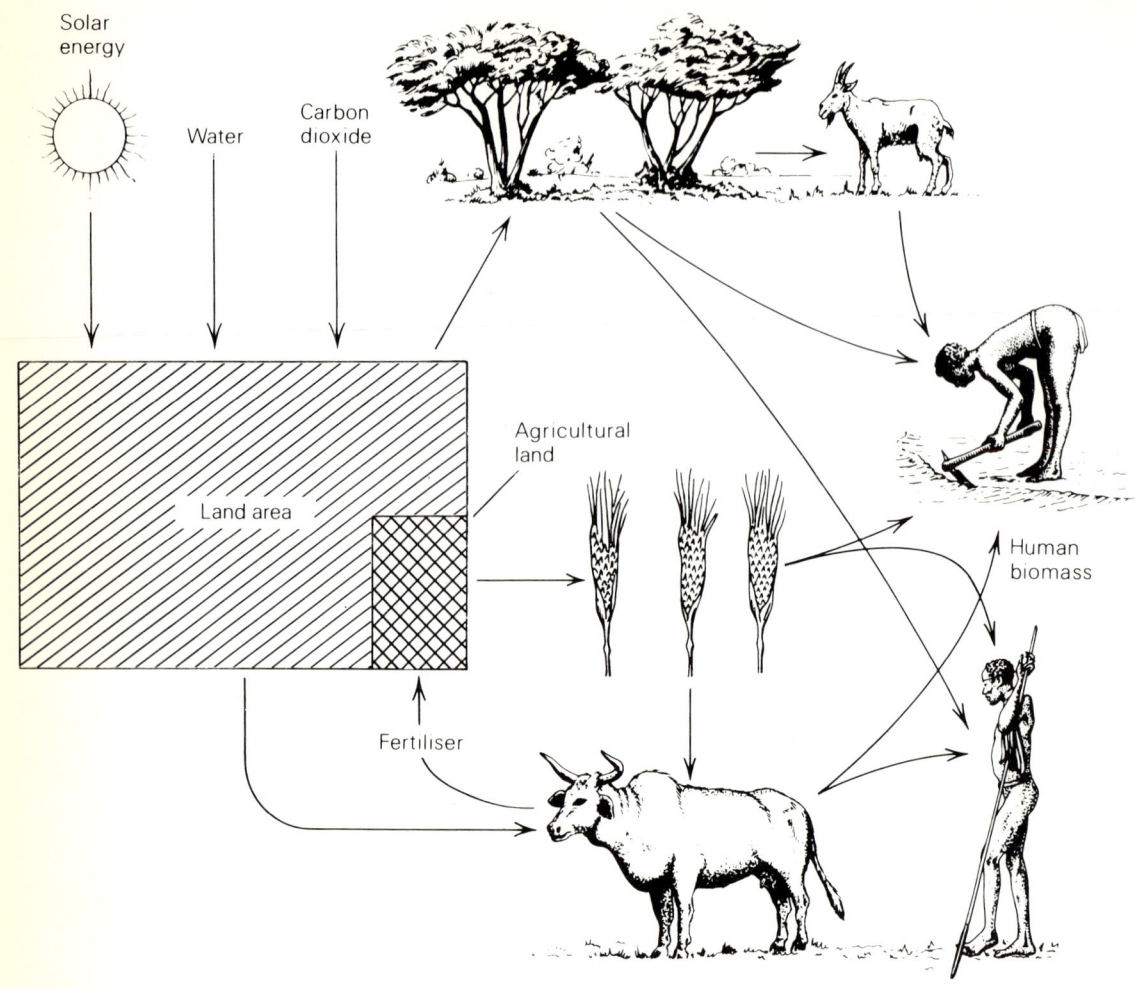

vegetation canopy and the litter shed by it. Water infiltrates less readily, accumulates on the surface and runs downslope carrying soil particles into the streams. The stores of energy and nutrients are thereby depleted and are replenished less effectively by the altered plant cover that remains; the productivity of the ecosystem diminishes (Fig. 12). The responses by human land-users to this downgrading are expressed in their agricultural systems.

Agricultural systems
Shifting cultivation
One way of dealing with the reduction in productivity of an area to below an acceptable level is to abandon the impoverished land and move elsewhere. This is called shifting cultivation. Because these cultivators rely on the stored energy and nutrients in the land they till, the length of time a plot of earth can be used for crops is very short (Fig. 13). Cultivation is adapted to environmental conditions and plots are selected for their suitability for growing particular plants. After cultivation for about two years the plots are abandoned.

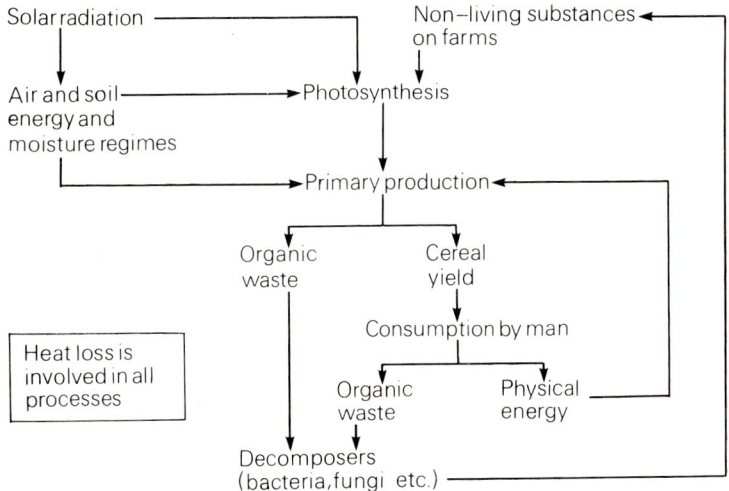

12 Energy flow in a simple farming system

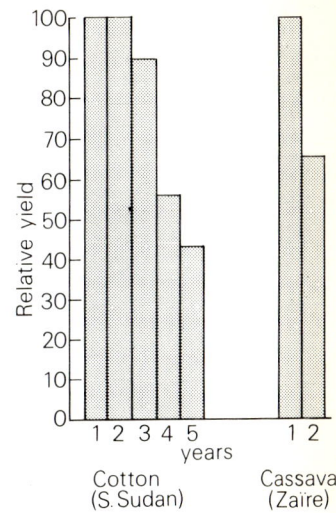

13 Decline in yields from trial fields under prolonged cropping in the humid African tropics under the system of shifting cultivation

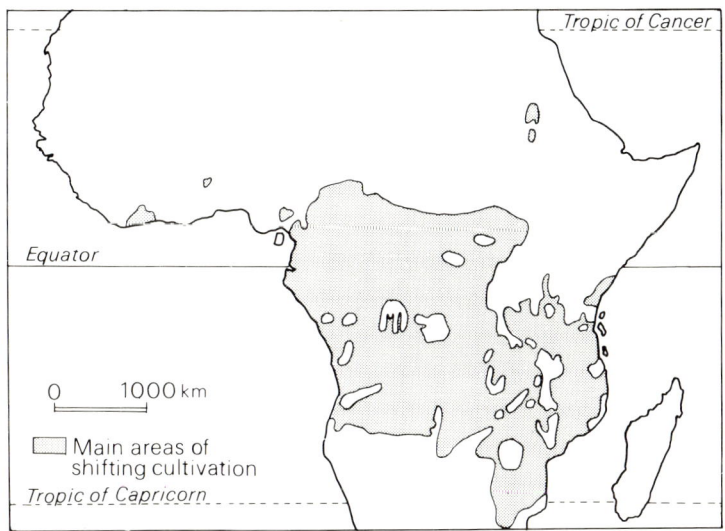

14 Distribution of the main areas of shifting cultivation in tropical Africa

The natural plant cover re-establishes itself and the energy and nutrient stores slowly build up again over a period of about twenty years. This span of time during which the vegetation re-establishes itself can be called a fallow period. A great deal of cultivable land must be available if this kind of agricultural system is going to work successfully, since new land has to be opened up for cultivation every two years at least and abandoned land cannot be re-used for more than twenty years. For instance, if 2 hectares of land are needed to grow crops for one person for two years, then 22 hectares of cultivable land are necessary for one person for the whole cultivation and fallow cycle. Not all land is cultivable, so the total land requirement could be very great.

As new land is continually being opened up, it is frequently necessary to move the settlements; otherwise the distance from the fields to the houses becomes too great. As such large amounts of cultivable land are needed to support each person and the villages have to be moved frequently, settlements tend to be small and trade between them restricted. Individual rights over pieces of land, once cropping has ceased, do not generally exist since the cultivator may never till the same piece of land again. Shifting cultivation was once a common form of land use in tropical Africa, when there were fewer people. Nowadays it is becoming less common but it still occurs in parts of central and east Africa (Fig. 14) where population densities are no more than 10 persons per sq. km.

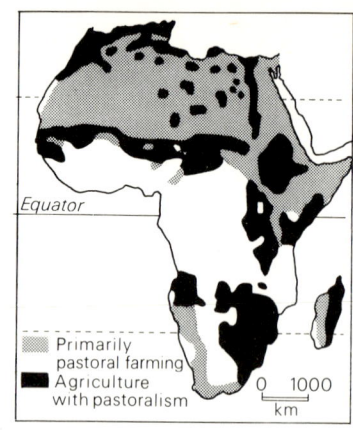

15 Distribution of pastoral activities in Africa

Nomadic pastoralism

A comparable mobility of life style is common among livestock farmers. The nomadic herdsmen (Fig. 15) and their animals search for rich and nutritious grazing, water supplies and salt. When they have exhausted the supply in one area they move on to fresh pastures. Since the herders are concerned with the availability of pastures throughout the year, the time scale for their movements is very different from that of the shifting cultivators. They follow an annual cycle. Pastoral nomads follow patterns of movement which remain fairly consistent from year to year since they like to stay in areas they know well. They tend to return every year to particular localities, their home bases, and thus their nomadic routes form circuits. Pastoralists are attracted by areas of permanent settlement where they can buy cereal foods and sell their produce, but grazing land is limited near villages because of cultivation by the local residents. The presence of pests, diseases and rival herdsmen deter movement in some directions. The nomads weigh up the relative importance of these various factors and move accordingly. Local circumstances determine the frequency, speed, distance and direction of movement each week. Occasionally severe conditions of drought, such as occurred in west Africa in 1973, or political troubles force the nomads to make major changes in their circuits.

Settled cultivation

Rotational fallow cultivation. Where it is no longer possible for people to keep moving to uncultivated land because there is just not sufficient land available, other ways of dealing with the maintenance of soil fertility have been devised. In some cases the cultivators live in areas where natural conditions are more favourable to crop growth but in other cases the increasing size of the population has stimulated technological innovations to overcome the problems. The most widespread form of agricultural practice in tropical Africa involves short periods of cultivation followed by periods of fallow (Fig. 16). The fallow period is not as long as that left by the shifting cultivators and the natural ecosystems are not allowed to re-establish themselves completely. At any one time in any one area, however, more land is under fallow than under cultivation. This kind of agricultural system is called rotational fallow cultivation. Fig. 17 shows where it occurs. It is found particularly in the savanna areas and can support densities of up to 250 persons per sq. km.

Apart from the fallow there are other practices which the rotational fallow cultivator employs in order to make the most use of the natural conditions and to lessen the impact both of the

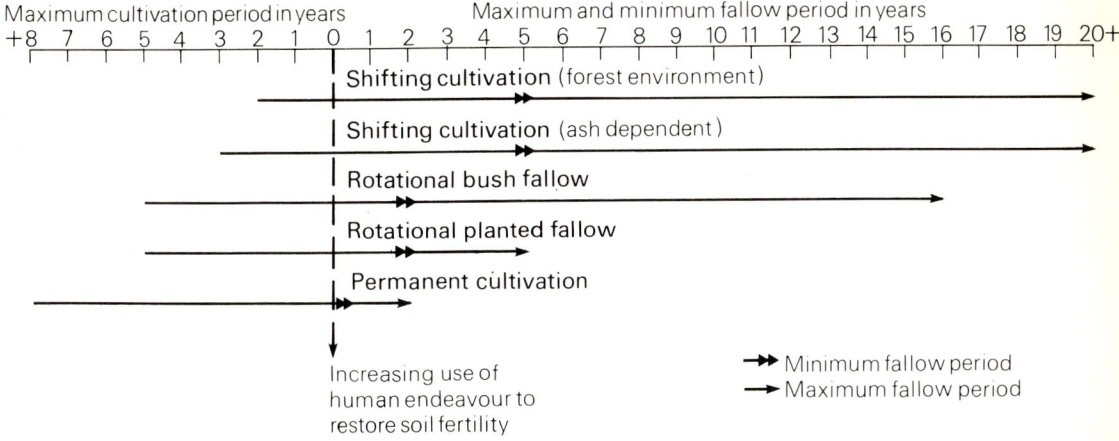

16 Some systems of land rotation in tropical Africa

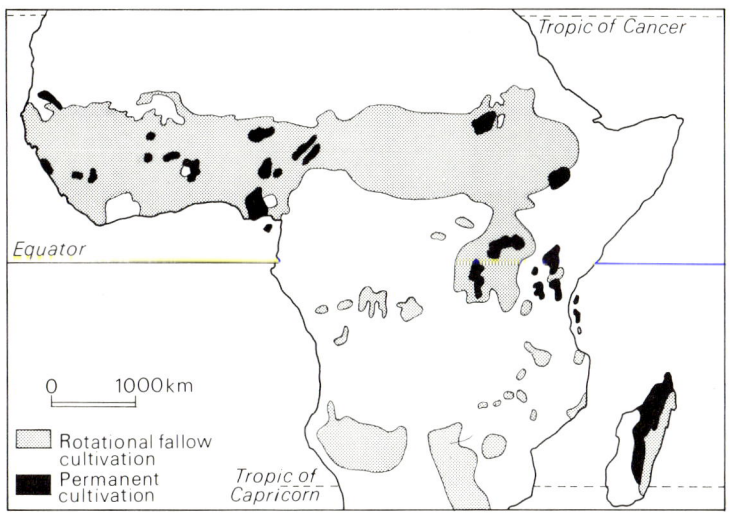

17 Distribution of main areas of rotational fallowing and permanent cultivation in tropical Africa

removal of some of the vegetation and the removal of the crops themselves, which in a natural state would remain where they had grown and hence within the system. The land close to the houses is frequently enriched with household waste, crop residues and manure from the free-ranging sheep, goats and poultry found in every village. To a large extent this replaces the nutrients removed in the crops. In these particularly favoured areas, usually known as gardens, which are cultivated continuously without a fallow period, special crops are grown. These crops may be ones that make large demands on soil nutrients, or require constant attention during growth, or be used frequently in cooking. In contrast the main fields, where the staple crops are grown, lie farther from the village and receive much less attention.

In the fields, different kinds of crops are grown on the same piece of land. Several crops may be grown together as a crop association; or they may be grown one after the other during one year – a crop sequence; or they may be grown one after the other over several years — a crop succession. Each crop takes its own particular requirements from the soil; the cultivator, by simulating the diversity of the natural vegetation associations, is causing a more balanced depletion of the soil nutrients as well as maintaining a protective vegetative cover over the soil. A further advantage of this practice to the farmer is the spreading of the work-load over a wider time period. The mixing of the crops also discourages the rapid spread of diseases which can ravage single stands. A wide range of crops is grown. In this way the farmer should be able to produce some food every year, for if conditions are unfavourable for one crop it is unlikely that they will be unfavourable for all. Which combinations of crops are grown depends on the specific ecological conditions in any particular area. In general grain crops such as *Sorghum* spp. and millets (*Eleusine* spp. and *Pennisetum* spp.) are common in the arid and savanna areas, and root crops such as yams (*Dioscorea* spp.) and tree crops are more common in the forest areas.

Other techniques employed to overcome disadvantages in the natural environment include irrigation by gravity flow channels or devices for raising water such as the shaduf, and the heaping of the soil into mounds or ridges to increase the amount of soil available to a plant in a particular place. All these techniques involve the concentration of energy and nutrients from a wide area into a smaller cultivated area. Very occasionally, they include the use of materials imported from considerable distances, while a small proportion of the crops may be exported to distant places. Most of the produce is for local consumption. With this form of agriculture, people are able to concentrate in larger settlements which remain fixed in one area for long periods of time. Communications are developed more extensively and trading, both locally and regionally, takes place. Gardens and field plots which are cultivated regularly are marked out and the farmers retain rights over plots of land even during the fallow period. There may also be land further from the village which is cleared occasionally and which members of the community, when in need, can use.

The population densities associated with rotational fallow cultivation are fairly large — up to 250 persons per sq. km — and in the long run the system is detrimental to the maintenance of soil fertility. Many farm economists consider that it represents a transitional phase between shifting cultivation and permanent cultivation. They would like to see the system improved by the farmers planting special fallow crops, which would be more productive than allowing natural regeneration, using more fertilisers and some machinery. All these improvements would require considerable investment by the farmers themselves and in general the prices the producers receive for their commercial crops are too low to provide either capital, the security necessary for credit or the incentive for radical change. Any improvements of this kind would also require profound alterations in the system of land tenure, the social customs and the general agricultural activities of complete groups of people, if they were to be in any way effective. Most progress is being made in countries like Nigeria, where funds from oil are available for purchasing fertilisers and equipment from overseas.

Permanent cultivation. In a limited number of areas in tropical Africa the fields as well as the gardens are cultivated every year; this is called permanent cultivation (see Fig. 17). In such places the natural ecosystems have been replaced by a system regulated by man. To keep land under cultivation year after year usually requires much effort by the farmers, although they do not have to do the heavy work of clearing new land for cultivation which plays a large part in the work-load of shifting and rotational fallow cultivators. Permanent cultivation is often found in areas where the environment is particularly favourable such as fertile volcanic soils, or land liable to seasonal flooding, or places where perennial crops can be grown. In these areas either the soil has considerable reserves of nutrients or these reserves are continually being renewed, as happens when silt is deposited on land during flooding. The ancient cultivation of the banks of the River Nile was possible because of the annual replacement of topsoil by floodwater. Under perennial crops the cultivation system is more akin to a natural ecosystem, since only the actual harvested produce is removed from the area. The leaf fall continues to replenish the supply of soil nutrients and the continuous vegetation canopy protects the soil from damage by heat or torrential storms.

Some continuous cultivation is also undertaken in areas with high population densities where cultivable land is scarce. Here farmers make use of numerous techniques to maintain soil fertility. They use any animal and vegetable manure available, build terraces or retaining walls to support a sufficient depth of soil, control water supplies to the fields, give careful attention to the needs of the growing plants and protect the crops from pests, diseases and predators. Much human energy is expended in operating this system and there is a greater degree of concentration of resources from a wide area into a smaller cultivated area than in the other kinds of farming. The yields per hectare are greater under permanent cultivation than under the other systems but output per man hour worked is said to be less, although the figures that are available are inconclusive. It is not easy to compare figures given for the amounts of work done by groups of people since often they do not contain precise details about the number of hours involved or the actual intensity of the work. There is evidence that where people have been able to move from areas of high population density and permanent cultivation to areas with plenty of land, they tend to revert to rotational fallow methods of cultivation. In part, however, this may be a reflection of differences in soil fertility between the areas concerned.

Some permanent cultivators use advanced techniques to produce goods for the world commercial market. At this level the inputs are numerous and complex and frequently come from outside Africa altogether, and the produce itself is usually exported outside Africa as well. Specialisation in specific crops such as cotton, groundnuts, coffee and pyrethrum is a feature of this kind of farming. This means that care has to be taken to replace the specific nutrients required by the particular crops — hence costly artificial fertilisers are used. Single stands of crops are readily attacked by pests and diseases, so pesticides and devices to repel predators are required. To

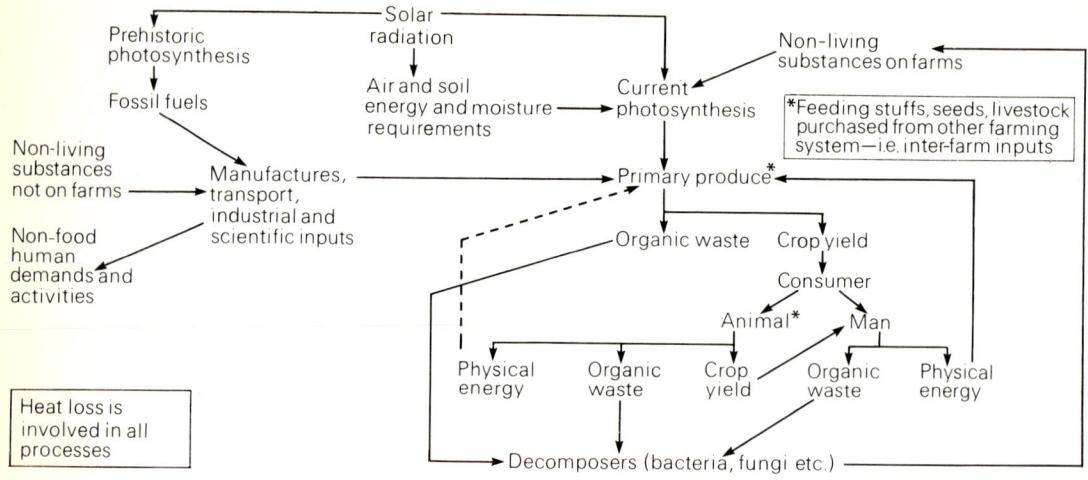

18 Energy flow in a complex farming system

be successful commercially the farmers often have to plant very large areas with one crop, and machinery is necessary in order to cope with the crop and complete each of the various activities at the optimum time. If too long a time is taken in sowing the crop it could mean that some of the seeds are unable to take advantage of the best conditions and thus do not grow as well as possible; taking too long to harvest a crop could mean that it becomes spoiled and therefore of less value when sold. Machinery is costly to purchase and requires fossil fuels, technical knowledge and spare parts to operate. In such a system the natural complexity is reduced but the application of imported energy and technical expertise is increased. The movement of nutrients and energy involved in such a commercial African ecosystem is also part of a global circulation involving international trade (Fig. 18).

Ethnic differentiation

The natural environment provides a base on which man operates (Fig. 19). The kind of response which man makes to the physical and biological conditions of the area he inhabits depends on the culture of the group to which he belongs. He views the world in terms of the traditions, customs, language and values of his ethnic group. In Africa ethnic groups are an important feature. Although population mobility is increasing most ethnic groups have territories which, at least in their core areas, can be readily identified and mapped. Each ethnic group has its own particular style of building, village layout, land tenure, land use and agricultural practices. The case studies related in the following chapters are examples of the variety of life styles in tropical Africa. In some areas it is possible to find examples of the whole range of agricultural systems from hunting to vast commercial plantations within a few kilometres of each other. Within an ethnic group, not every family will live and work in the same way. There is always a good deal of variation in individual aspirations and ways of life. The Pokot (Suk) of Kenya, for instance, are mainly semi-nomadic herdsmen but some cultivate land intensively, using irrigation. Amongst the Fulani of west Africa there are

Environment \ Man	Ecosystems			
	Tropical forest	Savanna	Arid	Montane etc.
Agricultural systems — Subsistence	Shifting cultivation in Zaïre (Sakata)	Shifting cultivation in Zambia (Bemba)	Nomadic pastoralism in Somalia (Somali)	Intensive hill farming in Togo (Kabrai)
Agricultural systems — Commercial	Rubber plantations in Liberia	Beef ranching in Rhodesia	Irrigated cotton in the Gezira, Sudan	Coffee farming in Tanzania (Chagga)

both sedentary cultivators and nomadic pastoralists. In any one group of people, some may cultivate commercially and others for subsistence, some may be rich and others poor, some may be reformers and others traditionalists.

Subsistence agriculture

Most rural people in tropical Africa are subsistence producers — that is they farm land or herd stock primarily to provide food for themselves and their families, though a little produce is often sold to raise cash to pay state taxes or school fees. There is no really clear-cut division between subsistence and commercial farming since many commercial farmers have fields set aside for growing their own food but, in general, commercial farmers are primarily engaged in raising produce to sell, whereas subsistence farmers are primarily engaged in raising produce they will consume themselves. For the subsistence farmer it is very important that he grow sufficient food for himself and his family every year, for without it there is no guarantee that they will not starve. The very nature of subsistence production means that the producers and the consumers are the same people, and money has only a limited importance. Security in the form of food is the major objective, not the making of the largest cash profit possible. The inputs involved in subsistence farming are usually limited to land, simple tools and work by the farmer and his family; hence the nature of the local environment and the risks associated with it are very important. The farmers spread these risks as widely as possible by cultivating a range of crops which tolerate different soil and weather conditions so that if some fail others may not be affected, or by moving from place to place as the nomadic herders do. The strategy of the individual farmer is based on his experience and his view of the situation. The actual type of production therefore varies from place to place and changes over time (Fig. 20). The resistance of farmers to new methods of production reflects the importance they attach to producing enough food every year. New methods, which appear to the outsider to be improvements on the old, may give larger yields in some years but none at all in others

20 Factors affecting the type of subsistence production

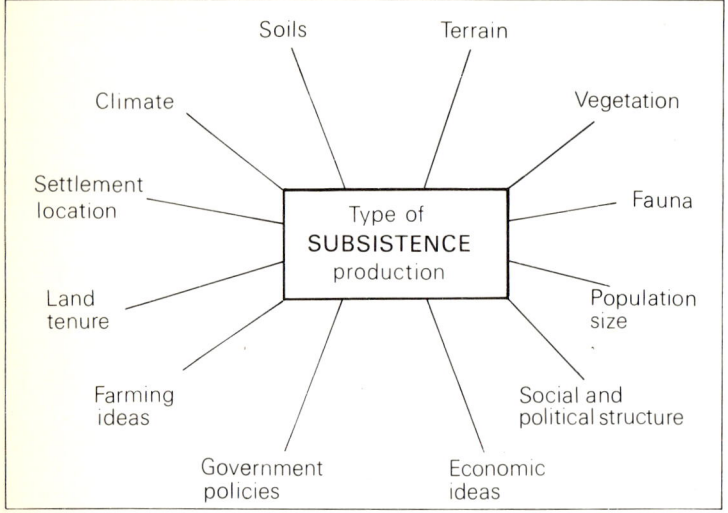

and the latter could mean starvation for those concerned. Similarly, employment for wages or the growing of crops to sell are frequently considered less important than the production of sufficient food and are only undertaken when spare time is available. For instance, the Azande men now grow cotton (*Gossypium* spp.) to sell as they no longer have to defend their territory against invaders and traditionally the women grow the food crops.

Land in many areas is readily available and personal ownership of land is not common. Most people are able to obtain land to cultivate from the head of their family or village and any payments for it are very small or related to the quantity of crops produced. The cultivators do not own the land they till but they are entitled to any crops they grow on it. This is called a cultivation or usufructury right. Renting or purchasing land, however, is found increasingly in areas of commercial agriculture. In places where there are limited supplies of soil with particular qualities, several systems of land tenure may operate simultaneously. Around the Mandinka village of Genieri in the Gambia, for instance, strict family ownership is maintained over the scarce ochre-brown sandy soils which are most suitable for growing groundnuts (*Arachis hypogaea*), whereas the remaining land is farmed under the more usual village-controlled cultivation right system.

The land farmed by a group of people does not usually form one compact area but consists of several small plots (each one often called a farm) situated in different places. In this way, given there is sufficient land available, the farmers can select plots with different soil conditions suitable for different kinds of crop. The plots may be several kilometres away from each other and from the farmers' houses. Plots are not hedged or fenced unless there is a need to protect the crops from animal damage. The spatial arrangements of farm land vary considerably but certain features recur. There are usually gardens close to the houses; here vegetables and herbs, which are used frequently in cooking, are grown. Further from the house are field plots where staple crops are grown. The gardens are manured and crops which need either much attention or particularly

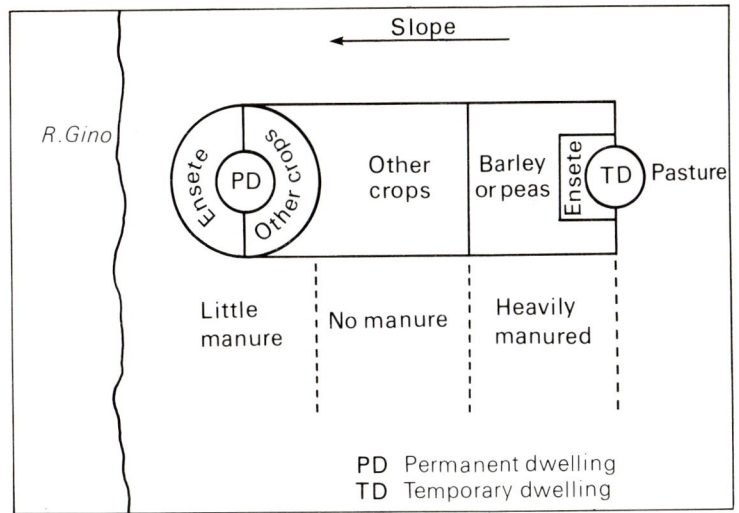

21 Generalised land use of a single holding among the richer Doko of the Gamu Highlands, Ethiopia, showing that land close to the temporary dwelling receives more manure than land close to the permanent dwelling

fertile soils are also grown there. When working on plots a long way from their homes the farmers frequently build temporary shelters to live in and save themselves the nightly trek back home. Sometimes areas close to these temporary settlements benefit from additional inputs, as Fig. 21 illustrates. The Doko live in a heavily populated (100 to 240 persons per sq. km), hilly part of Ethiopia. The richer farmers have several blocks of farm land, which may be one to two kilometres apart. To get from block to block involves several hours' travelling time, usually on foot. Because of the pressure of population on the land, the cattle can be grazed only on the hilltop pastures and, in order to save time and money, herdsmen are installed in temporary dwellings at the junction between the arable and the grazing land. The cattle are kept in stalls at night in the temporary dwellings and the manure collected in the cattle sheds is used on the land just below these outposts. (It is easier to carry the manure downhill than uphill.) As only one or two cattle are kept at the permanent homesteads less manure is available there. The cultivation of ensete (*Ensete edule*) is considered in detail in Chapter 6.

In most parts of Africa, farm land has not been difficult to obtain until comparatively recently, and techniques involving the use of artificial fertilisers and machinery which require capital for their purchase have not been well developed. In this kind of situation the labour of the farmer and his family is the most significant input. Farming units, that is groups of people farming together, vary in size both with ethnic group and within any community but, on average, the amount of land cultivated per person and per farm worker varies little, ranging from 0.2 to 0.8 hectares per person and 0.4 to 1.2 hectares per farm worker. The sizes of the land holdings are related to the number of farm workers in the household. The time spent on work is a very important consideration. Decisions about farming methods and produce to be raised are made, therefore, in terms of the work involved. Yields per unit of labour are a more significant measure for the farmer than yields per hectare. The subsistence cultivator aims to produce as large a crop as possible in relation to the work involved rather than to get as large a yield as possible from each hectare or as much profit as possible. It is very difficult, however, to measure work precisely, and valid comparisons of the work done by different groups are rare.

The seasonal nature of much of the work presents problems and the ability of the farmer and his assistants to cope with the busiest season often sets a limit on the area which they can cultivate effectively, even though they may appear to be doing little work at other times of the year. In relation to the inputs returns are high, but greater inputs of work, either in the form of cultivating larger areas or using more time-consuming intensive methods, do not necessarily result in proportionately greater outputs or greater cash returns. Furthermore production in surplus of family requirements may be difficult to sell for lack of buyers or transport or even lack of knowledge of places requiring extra food. An unsold surplus has no value except for entertaining friends and creating goodwill — which could be valuable later if times become hard. People who are generous when they have plenty are usually helped by friends and neighbours if they come to be in difficulties. The main ways in which the activities of subsistence producers vary are in the type of produce they raise and the amount of movement in their lives.

The tools used by subsistence farmers are few and very simple. The common ones are digging sticks, hoes, knives and machetes. They may be made from wood alone or have metal parts. Working with metal is a long-established traditional craft in Africa. Ploughs, however, have always been uncommon except in Ethiopia. The use of animal power in agriculture is not very widespread since in many areas oxen cannot be kept because of the likelihood of the disease trypanosomiasis, which is carried by tsetse flies. Animals are used for transport in the drier areas but chiefly as pack animals since the wheel was never developed in traditional tropical African technology.

It should not be forgotten that non-agricultural activities play an important part in rural life. Dwellings, storage bins and fences have to be built and kept in good repair; tools, furniture, household utensils, cloth, clothing and ornaments have to be made. Some groups of people like the Nupe and the Hausa are famous for the quality of their craftsmanship. Hunting wild animals and the collection of wild produce are also important seasonal pursuits and community activities which include weddings, funerals, religious rituals and the maintenance of good relations with all members of the family are vital and time-consuming. This sort of activity provides a network of social links which can be drawn on for assistance in times of difficulty: a form of social insurance.

A large family unit, consisting of several generations, may live together in separate dwellings within one large compound. This family unit may have rights over land as a group but the normal farming unit, that is those people working together on the land, usually consists of only one man and his immediate family. At particular times this unit may include more distant relatives or hired help. The roles of men and women often differ. Among cattle herders, men frequently look after the animals and women the production and distribution of milk. Among cultivators, men undertake the heavy work of clearing the land for tillage whilst women weed and harvest. Children assist from an early age. If the need for extra labour is particularly great at some stage, labourers may be hired or local people invited to help in return for food and drink, possibly with musical accompaniment to the work.

Some form of redistribution of goods is common at the local level, particularly where different kinds of produce are available in one area. This may result from variations in the local environment or the juxtaposition of different types of agricultural activity such as herding and cultivating. Movement of goods and people within and between the ecological zones is discussed in the final chapter.

Commercial agriculture

Commercial agriculture is less closely linked with the natural environment than is subsistence agriculture. Whereas the subsistence cultivator makes use of his surroundings to provide himself with food, the commercial cultivator uses the land to make a monetary profit. Economic and political considerations become more important in the decisions he takes than do the small-scale variations in soil and vegetation on his land. The physical environment, however, is still a factor in the pattern of commercial agriculture since the climatic range over the continent sets limits on areas where specific crops can be cultivated to best advantage and at least cost. Hence the major production of cocoa (*Theobroma cacao*) and oil palms (*Elaeis guineensis*) is in the forest zone and cotton and groundnuts in the savanna. At the level of the individual country, the influence of the environment can be seen in the limit of the cocoa belt within the forest zone of Ghana (see Fig. 37, p. 43) or the altitudinal crop zones in Kenya (see Fig. 70, p. 82). Many of the commercially important plants have been introduced into Africa from elsewhere, notably cocoa, *Hevea* rubber, maize (*Zea mays*) and cassava (*Manihot utilissima*). The Portuguese were responsible for bringing many new plants to tropical Africa from the Americas. Local research institutes have developed special varieties of export crops with a view to increasing yields and improving resistance to disease, thus overcoming some of the environmental problems. The commercial farmers vary in the complexity of their operations but they rely heavily on imported machinery, fertilisers, pesticides and fossil fuels, as well as the existence of good lines of communication and water supply. The kinds of machinery used range from the knapsack pesticide spray of the cocoa farmer to the large combine harvester of the Rhodesian wheat farmer.

Commercial agriculture in tropical Africa is directed, in the main, towards supplying primary produce to other parts of the world, particularly North America, Europe and Japan, and only secondarily with supplying foodstuffs for its own people and raw materials for its own industries. Transport costs play a significant part in determining the location of different kinds of agriculture. Areas of commercial agriculture in Africa are associated with areas which have relatively well-developed networks of communications. In many countries such as Kenya, Rhodesia, Tanzania, Zaïre and Zambia commercial activity is concentrated along the railway lines. Today, the building of a railway line does not stimulate automatically the development of commercial agriculture in the same way that it did at the turn of the century when railways were the prime mode of

22 Range of variations in the major features of commercial agriculture in tropical Africa

Organisation	Labour force	Capital expenditure	Land alienation	Government policy
Plantation with associated smallholdings	Many permanent employees	Much capital expenditure on land, machinery, irrigation works etc.	Sale of land to foreigners and non-Africans	Direct management of agriculture
Plantation				Management by special boards or public enterprises
Estate	Few permanent employees		Land concessions to foreigners for plantations and estates	Settlement schemes
	Seasonal employees			Land tenure schemes
Farm			Agricultural land rented to foreigners	Permissive acts, e.g. Marketing Boards, Research Institutes
Smallholding	Family labour only	Little capital expenditure	No sale of land to foreigners	*Laissez-faire*

transport. Areas which were favoured by improved accessibility at an early date, however, have taken advantage of this lead and remain important commercially. In south-west Nigeria the extension eastwards of the planting of cocoa trees was partially associated with the development of the road system, and road networks are generally more significant in the development of areas of commercial agriculture nowadays. Lack of good communications prevents the marketing of surplus produce away from the area in which it is grown. Many problems of food shortage are associated with distribution difficulties rather than the failure of production. The development of communications and marketing will be considered in greater detail in Chapter 7.

National differentiation

The political experiences of the various African states have contributed significantly to the patterns of organisation of commercial agriculture (Fig. 22). During colonial times, in Nigeria, for instance, the sale of land to foreigners was discouraged, while in countries like Cameroun and Zaïre foreign companies were permitted to acquire large areas of land for plantations, and in Kenya, Rhodesia, Angola and Mozambique settlement by Europeans was encouraged. Present-day African commercial agriculture, therefore, covers the range from small-scale peasant production to large capital-intensive plantations usually owned by foreign companies employing foreign nationals as managers and a local wage-earning labour force. As governments are able to raise money by taxes or international loans, they are important sources of capital for the development of commercial agriculture. They finance irrigation and drainage works, changes in land tenure, improved or new transport networks, marketing organisations and research into crop varieties and methods of cultivation. Not all capital comes from the government, however, for the early cocoa farmers in Ghana built their own roads and bridges to improve communications as well as invested their profits in the purchase of more land. Individual capital accumulation is linked

23 Land use around Addis Ababa, Ethiopia

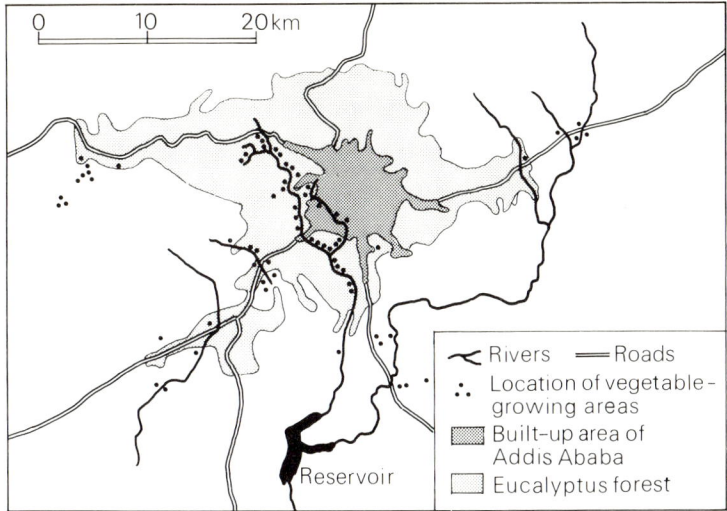

with the proximity of a substantial market for crops and the possibility of earning cash from urban employment. The rise of commercial farming in Buganda was associated with the existence of a market for plantains and cotton in Kampala and Jinja, together with employment opportunities there. Other features contributing to the growth of commercial agriculture in Buganda were the distinctive land tenure system of individual ownership known as the *mailo* system, which was introduced by the colonial administration in 1900; the availability of immigrant labour to work the farms; and the construction of a metalled road network in the Kampala area after the 1914–18 War. Zones of market gardening and commercial food production have developed around urban (Fig. 23) and mining centres and areas of concentrated export crop production such as the Gezira in the Sudan.

Over the continent as a whole, commercial agriculture has increased in both area and total production. The volume of production and the quantities of specific commodities exported by individual states vary each year. Over longer periods the relative importance of producing areas also changes. Local weather conditions, diseases, the price paid to producers, the amount of produce required for domestic consumption and the markets open to the individual countries all have their influence. Some commodities, such as cocoa and formerly coffee (*Coffea* spp.), have their production limited to some degree by international quota agreements, whilst some countries have especially advantageous trading links such as the association between the countries of the Lomé Trade and Aid Convention and the European Economic Community.

Although the area under major crops in Africa increased by 40% between 1950 and 1970, from 67 400 000 hectares to 94 700 000 hectares, significant commercial agriculture is still concentrated in limited areas. Generally, these have experienced the cumulative advantages, in comparison with other African areas, of an early development of mechanised transport, an early introduction to commercial and export potentials and a response from the local

24 Sale price of 'mailo' land in Buganda, 1959–65

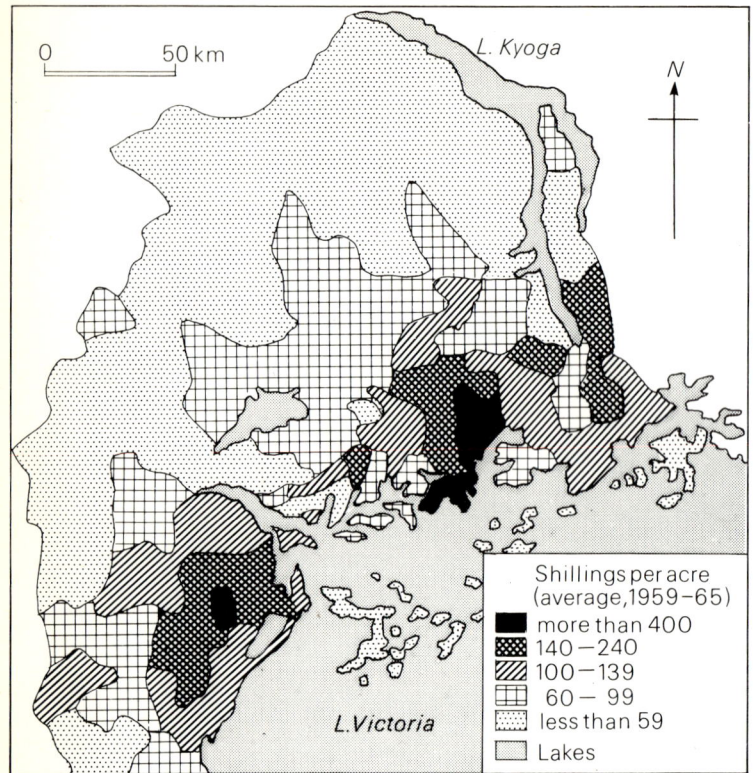

people to these possibilities. These areas contain a large proportion of the wealth of the individual countries and facilities like motor vehicles, piped water supplies, schools and hospitals. Where there are commercial activities in rural areas, economic forces are becoming significant, particularly in bringing about a recognition of the specific value of land as it becomes scarcer, and generating a market in it. For instance, in Ahafo, a cocoa boom area in Ghana, non-Ahafo people have paid rent for cocoa land since about 1912, demonstrating that it was recognised as an economic asset at an early date; while in Buganda, the sale price in the 1960s of the privately owned *mailo* land decreased away from the major town of Kampala and the shore of Lake Victoria. *Mailo* land no longer exists in Buganda (Fig. 24).

3

The humid forest lands

High forest covers much of the Zaïre basin between the Atlantic and the western arm of the rift valley between Uganda and Zaïre and also along the Guinea coast (Fig. 25). In this area the mean annual rainfall exceeds 1400 mm and on average in no more than two months does less than 100 mm of rain fall. Evapo-transpiration losses are only moderately high throughout the year. The majority of the plant species in the forest are evergreen trees but the proportion of deciduous trees increases towards the drier margins. The flora contains a large number of different species, up to forty per hectare. The west African rain forest is reckoned to contain some 7000 different species altogether, but this is less than is found in the forests of tropical south America and south-east Asia. A possible explanation

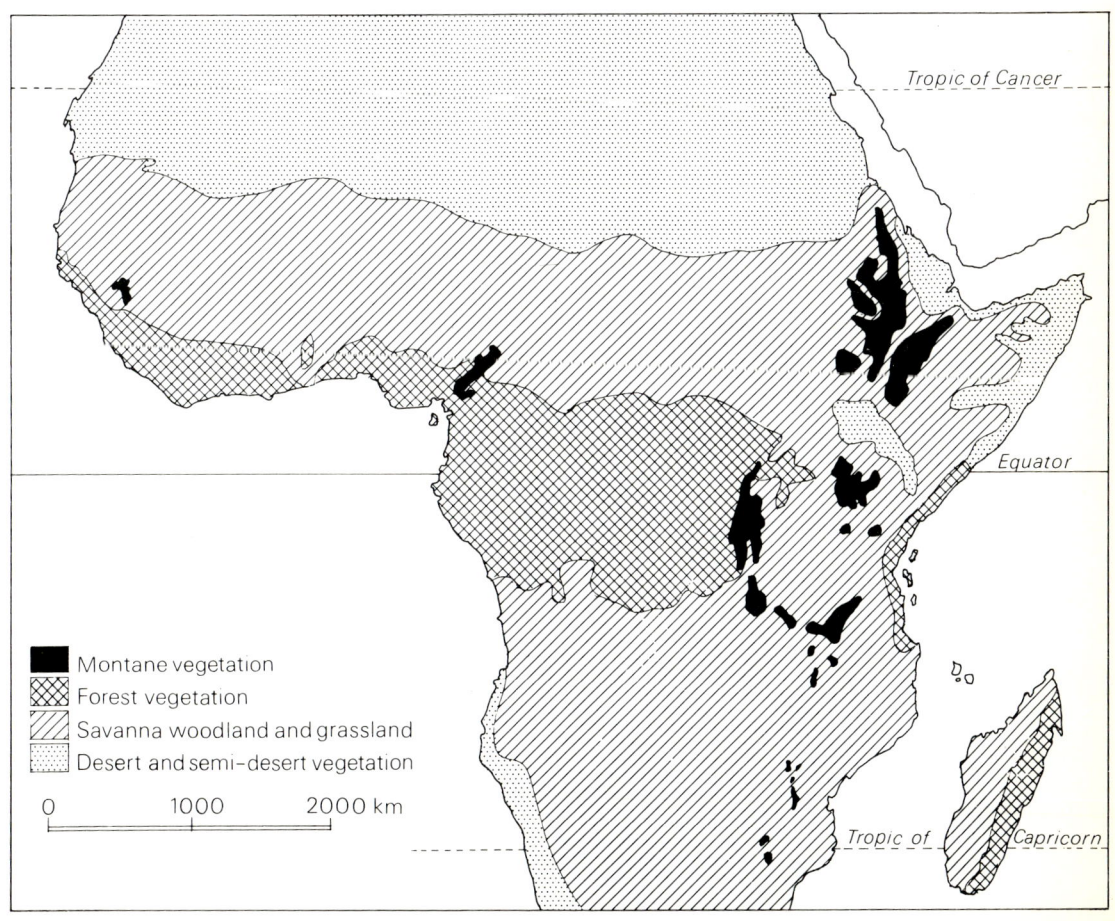

25 Distribution of major vegetation types in tropical Africa

26 Differing tree levels in tropical forest in southern Nigeria

for the lesser number of species in humid tropical Africa is that aridity in the glacial stages of the last Ice Age may have reduced the extent of lowland rain forest to a few, quite limited, areas from which it has since expanded.

The forest trees such as African mahogany (*Khaya* spp.), iroko (*Chlorophora excelsa*) and afara (*Terminalis* spp.) have straight trunks, thin, smooth bark and are shallow rooted, often with buttresses at the base. The main leafy canopy is 20 to 30 metres above the ground with the crowns of individual trees emerging above it. There are one or two other layers at lower levels (Fig. 26). Climbing lianas and parasitic plants (epiphytes) are abundant but the forest floor, deep in shade, is fairly bare. There are few shrubs and herbs. About half the forest plant species are between 8 and 30 metres tall and the crowns of the tallest trees tend to be much broader than those at lower levels. The animal, bird, insect and reptile population of the forest shows a similar richness in the number of species. Each level in the forest has its own particular set of inhabitants.

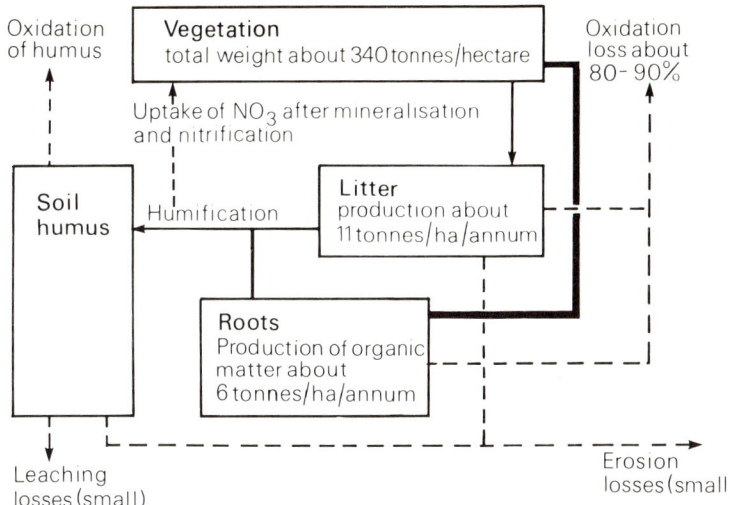

27 Organic-matter relationships under tropical forest
The total weight of roots might be put at say 100 tonnes/hectare

The biomass of tropical forest is very great, about 450 tonnes per hectare. Although there is an abundance of vegetative matter in storage as leaves and trunks and the amount of litter produced is massive, organic matter does not accumulate in the upper layers of the soil to any great extent (Fig. 27). This is because the bacteria responsible for the decomposition of the litter are very active, and breakdown is swift. The nutrients are re-cycled through the plants and animals almost continuously in what is virtually a closed system. In general the soil material is highly weathered, free-draining and acidic. The soils are called *latosols* and they vary in colour from yellow in the wettest areas to red-brown in the drier ones. The soil profiles often include a layer of hard, iron-rich material called lateritic ironstone.

At the drier margins of the forest the trees are not quite so tall and many lack buttresses. Some lose their leaves in the dry season and may flower at that time of year. In Africa much of the drier forest has been cleared for cultivation and little remains.

Within the forest itself, that is within and beneath the vegetation canopy, the climate is significantly different from that existing above the trees. The canopy absorbs or reflects the sun's rays (insolation) and prevents temperatures reaching high values. A lower, more even, temperature exists within the forest; fluctuations tend to be less than those outside and to lag behind them. Forest soils have an almost constant temperature, with a daily amplitude of only 1 or 2 °C at a depth of 20 cm. The tree canopy also shields the forest floor from the impact of rainfall, which is intense and heavy in the tropics. Also it supplies much water vapour to the atmosphere through evaporation and transpiration. The humidity within the forest is high and any variations tend to be small and lag behind the ones outside.

Hunting and gathering

The humid forests of the Ituri Basin in north-east Zaïre are the home of Pygmy people. These people live by moving from place to place collecting snails, termites and the larvae of moths. They also gather

28 Pygmy people beside their houses in the forest

fruits, berries and nuts, and hunt and trap small animals using nets or bows and arrows. The Pygmies leave the forest ecosystem relatively undisturbed. Ideally a band of twenty Pygmies needs about 500 sq. km of forest to support itself; there are about 35 000 Pygmies in the whole region. Although the Pygmies know about fire they do not use it to clear vegetation (Fig. 28).

Cultivation

The Sakata

Other forest dwellers, however, use fire and stone tools to clear patches of forest for cultivation. It is easier to clear land on the drier margins of the forest where the vegetation is less dense and the sun can penetrate more easily. Forest people such as the Sakata of Zaïre plant vegetables, maize, tobacco (*Nicotiana* spp.), plantains (*Musa* spp.) and sweet potatoes (*Ipomoea batatas*) in small gardens around their houses. Household waste is put on these plots and the crops are protected from the depredations of monkeys and other animals. During the dry season, from July to September, the Sakata clear other plots in the forest farther away from their homes. The vegetation is cut down with a machete and the debris is burned on the spot, thus providing some additional nutrients to the soil. Hardwoods and useful trees such as iroko, kola (*Cola* spp.) and oil palm are not cut down but are left standing. In the clearings, the Sakata

29 Cross-section diagrams of cultivation in the tropical forest of Zaïre

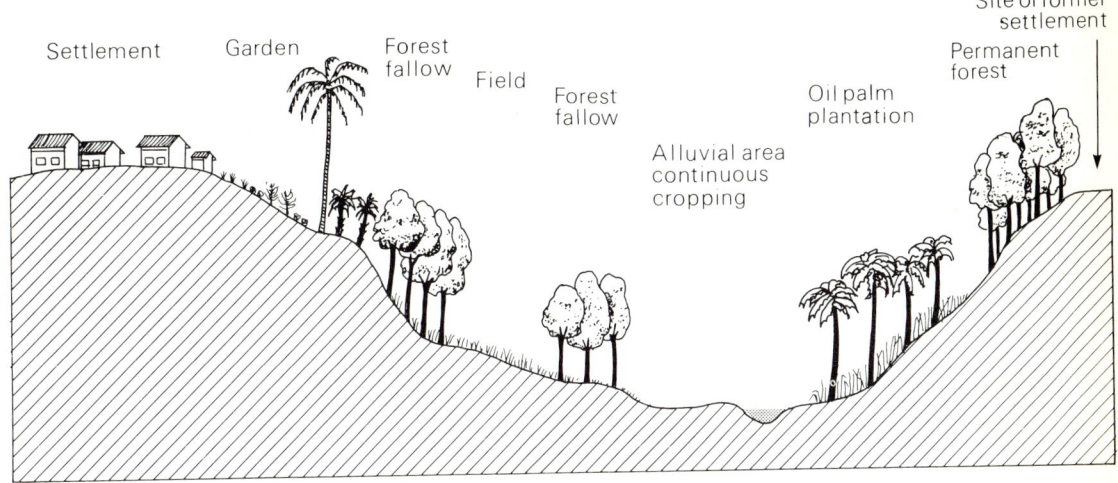

(a) Cross-section of village area

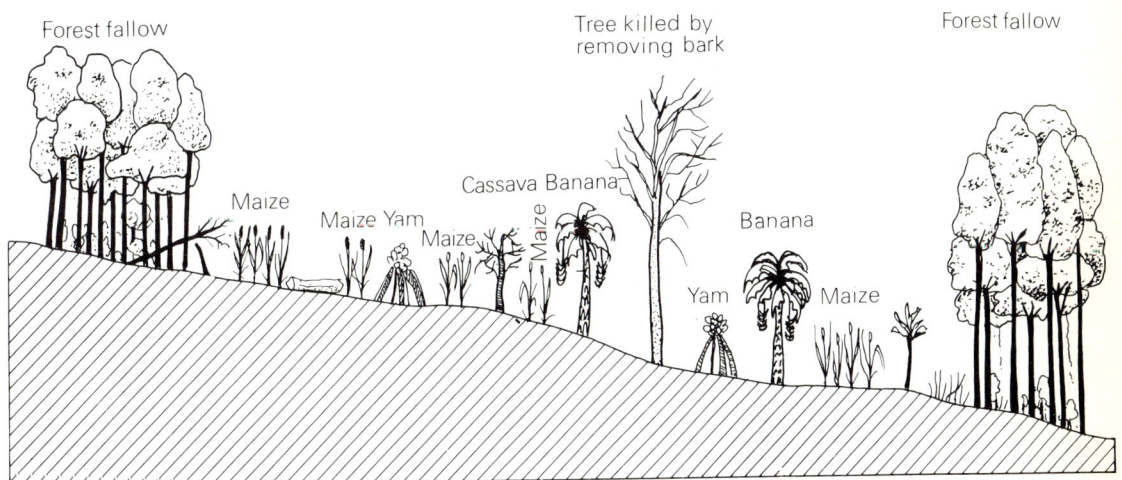

(b) Cross-section of a field

make mounds on which they grow cassava and in between they plant bananas (*Musa* spp.), plantains, maize and tobacco (Fig. 29). The plots look disorderly because a large variety of crops are grown together or in sequence. The aim of the Sakata is to obtain harvests of fresh food throughout the year thus making storage unnecessary, for in the humid climate stored crops deteriorate rapidly. Some crops, such as sugar-cane (*Saccharum officinarum*) and rice (*Oryza* spp.) are grown as pure stands in special plots where the soils are particularly moist and fertile. The interruption of the natural closed cycle of growth and decay causes soil fertility to decline. For a time crops thrive, so long as invading plants and weeds can be kept under control. Eventually these multiply excessively and nutrient stores in the soil diminish through the absence of leaf fall and the removal of the crops. Once the crops fail to grow healthily the clearing is abandoned and forest vegetation invades the area once more. The Sakata generally abandon plots after three years and move on to

30 Secondary forest in eastern Nigeria

clear other sites. The secondary forest which develops on the previously cultivated plots may look like the original vegetation but the combination of plants present (its floristic composition) is quite different from that of virgin forest. Softwood trees and plants considered useful, for their fruit or other purposes, are more numerous (Fig. 30). In areas where the density of population has increased, this secondary forest may be cleared once every fifteen years or less because of a shortage of alternative cultivable land.

In the forested areas it is difficult to find good examples of subsistence cultivators operating a rotational fallow cultivation. This is because the people of the forested areas of west Africa and Madagascar have had commercial contacts with other parts of the world for a long time and have developed the cultivation of perennial trees to provide cash crops for export. The rotational fallow cultivation of subsistence produce is, therefore, associated with a more permanent form of cash crop cultivation. Land under permanent tillage reduces the land available for growing food and, therefore, has a similar effect to that of increasing population densities. An area which has been planted with cocoa for forty years, however, cannot be replanted with cocoa for a further thirty years, so even this perennial cultivation is of a rotational fallow type but operating on a rather different time scale.

The Allada Yoruba and the Gouro
Frequently forest cultivators clear some plots for food crops and have other plots under perennial crops such as oil palms or coffee. A group of the Yoruba people who live in the Allada area of Benin (the majority of the Yoruba people live in Nigeria) cultivate plots of cassava and maize for about five years and then leave the plots to fallow for about seven years. Some of these people have less land

available than others and in this case the farmers let the land lie fallow for shorter periods and grow more cassava and maize. Cassava is a crop which can grow on poor soils and needs little attention during growth. The root is the part which is eaten but this does not need to be harvested until required; hence in good years some of the crop may not be wanted and will be left in the ground. Because cassava is such a reliable crop its popularity with farmers is increasing and it is grown in many areas as an insurance against the failure of other crops. Cassava, however, is a less nutritious food than most of the other cereal and root crops grown.

The Allada Yoruba spend most of their time growing food but they also derive an income from oil palms. In some parts of their area the oil palms are simply the dominant wild species remaining in forest which has been cleared and cultivated before. In other areas there are dense groves of planted oil palms. Once the trees are established there is little further work required other than harvesting the nuts and taking them to the crushing mill for the oil to be extracted. In the old days the oil was extracted by boiling or fermenting and pounding the nuts by hand. This extracted 45% to 55% of the available oil. Nowadays there are hand presses which can obtain up to 65% and power-operated crushing mills which express 85%. The oil extracted by mechanical means is purer and contains less free fatty acids, hence it attracts a higher price than the traditionally prepared oil.

The Gouro of the Ivory Coast, on the other hand, grow cassava, yams, groundnuts and beans (*Phaseolus* spp.) for food in their forest clearings. Yams, groundnuts and beans are harvested the same year but cassava plants take more than a year to grow to maturity so they are left in the soil while coffee is planted among them. The coffee plants then occupy the plot for up to thirty years and meanwhile other vegetation grows up round them.

The Betsimisaraka
In Madagascar the east coast is forested. Here the wet season lasts for about eleven months of the year and the annual rainfall is over 2500 mm. Where cultivation has taken place Traveller's trees (*Ravenala madagascariensis*) and bamboos (*Arundinaria* spp.) have become the dominant vegetation. The island is mountainous and in the area where the Betsimisaraka live the land drops rapidly from the interior mountains to the coast. The Betsimisaraka inhabit large villages perched on shelves above the narrow river valleys. Swamp rice is grown on the narrow valley floors but space is limited and the Betsimisaraka have not developed the complex irrigation techniques of the Betsileo who live in the interior of the island and cultivate irrigated swamp rice on a permanent basis. The Betsimisaraka clear the forest as well, to provide land for crops of upland rice, and they plant cocoyams (*Colocasia* spp.) round the edges of the plots. One year of cultivation is followed by about five years of fallow. Although the island is free from tsetse flies which carry the cattle disease trypanosomiasis, cattle do not thrive in the warm humid climate and hence are not kept. No manure, therefore, is available for the fields. Other food crops such as cassava, maize, sweet potatoes and beans are important and cash crops are grown. Coffee is the main cash

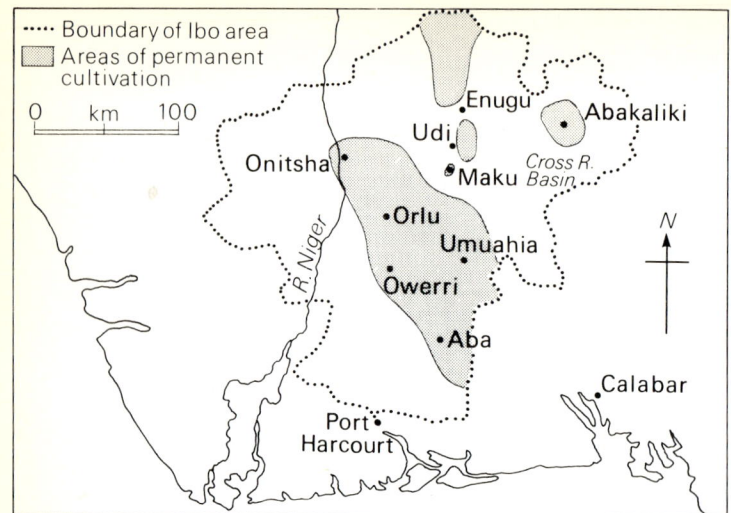

31 Distribution of permanent cultivation within the Ibo area of Nigeria

crop but vanilla (*Vanilla planifolia*), cloves (*Eugenia caryophyllata*), bananas and oriental fruits such as lychees (*Litchi chinensis*) grow well and are sold to buy food if the rice crop is insufficient.

The Ibo
In some formerly forested areas population densities are very high and the people are no longer able to leave land uncultivated for long periods. In these areas the forest is reduced to a mosaic of farms and scrub with tall trees remaining only on uncultivable slopes, in seasonal swamps or preserved in sacred groves. In many of these areas artificial fertilisers cannot be obtained for lack of money but the farmers have devised other methods so that cultivation can continue though under conditions of progressively declining soil fertility. In the Ibo area of Nigeria (Fig. 31) there are some very high population densities, exceeding 250 persons per sq. km. In the past the Ibo responded to population pressures by migrating westward across the River Niger and eastwards into the Cross River basin in search of more land, but the imposition of British rule at the beginning of the twentieth century prevented further expansion of their territory. Modern emigration is generally of people in search of wage employment in rural or urban areas rather than settlement on new land for cultivation.

Although there are now a number of towns in the Ibo area, most of the people are farmers. The typical Ibo settlement pattern is one of dispersed rural homesteads usually called compounds. These often contain a disproportionately high number of old and young people who are dependent to some extent on money sent home by town dwellers. The former forest has been cropped to such an extent that an artificial oil palm woodland has been created. Although oil palms are the most significant crop since the sale of the oil provides cash, the main staple crop is yam. Most families own land around their compounds to which they give most attention and care (Fig. 32). Sheep, goats and poultry are confined for part of the day in order to ensure supplies of manure which are composted with refuse and spread on this compound land. Tree crops such as oil palm, bananas, plantain, citrus fruits and kola nuts are grown here with cocoyams, cassava and vegetables (Fig. 33).

Plots which are further from the compound are called outer farms and may be owned by the family or worked under a cultivation

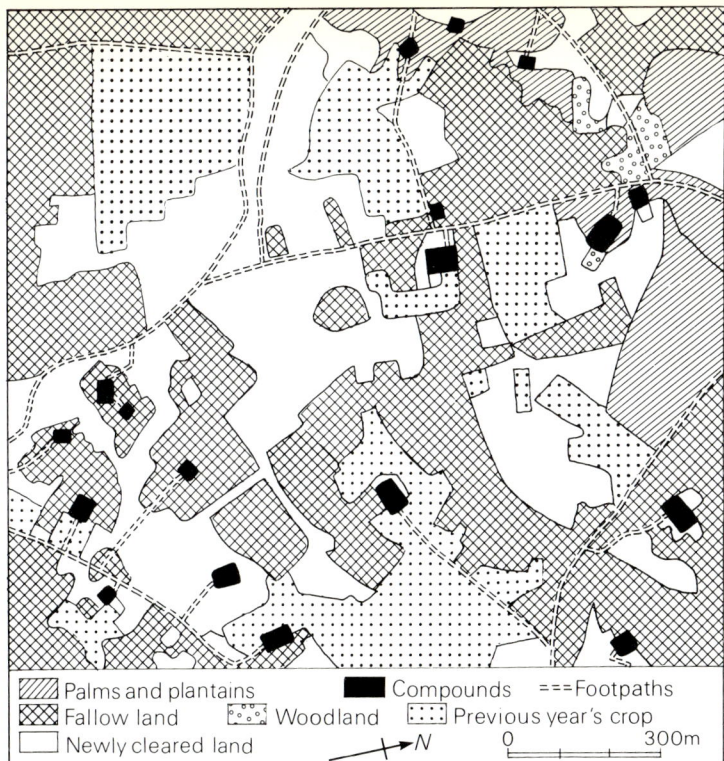

32 Settlement and land use near Aba, Nigeria

Key:
- Palms and plantains
- Fallow land
- Newly cleared land
- Compounds
- Woodland
- Footpaths
- Previous year's crop
- N   0   300m

right. These plots are also cropped continuously using crop sequences and short fallows. The staple yams are grown here on mounds. Yams provide high yields per hectare but they are demanding plants and cannot be grown on the same plot more frequently than once every three years (Table 3). Other crops are planted on the sides of the yam mounds and *Crotolaria*, a legume, is grown as a fallow crop to protect the soil. In areas where a longer fallow period is possible *Acioa barterii*, a small fast-maturing tree, is planted as a fallow crop. The trunks are used for firewood when the land is

33 Calendar of farming activities among the Ibo

	Jan	Feb	Mar	Apr	May	June	July	Aug	Sept	Oct	Nov	Dec
Men's work	Completion of yam harvest	Clearing bush if necessary		Planting late yam and cassava			Topping early yam				Barnwork	
	Barnwork	Planting early yam on compound land		Staking vines of early yam	Staking and training yam vines	Staking and training yam vines	Training yam vines		Planting cassava			
	Planting yellow yam	Planting yellow yam				Harvesting fresh maize	Harvesting fresh maize	Harvesting dry maize			Harvesting yam	Storing yam in barns
	Clearing bush if necessary		Making yam mounds for late yam crop				Planting cassava					Planting cassava
Women's work	Harvesting cocoyam			Planting maize, okra, fluted pumpkins, melons, cocoyam and cassava		W	e	e	d	i	n	g
	Planting new cassava					Planting cassava			Planting		cassava	
	Weeding old cassava	Planting maize and fluted pumpkins on compound land			Harvesting fresh maize from compound land	Harvesting fresh maize	Harvesting dry maize			Harvesting cocoyam		
			Planting groundnuts, making mounds for late yam crop				Harvesting groundnuts		Planting pepper on compound land			

Table 3. An example of typical crop associations and sequences in the use of three fields over six years, near Nnewi

Year	Field 1	Field 2	Field 3
1	Yams Beans (*Phaseolus* sp.) Vegetables	Cassava Pigeon peas (*Cajanus cajan*)/Cucurbits Fallow (*Crotolaria*)	Maize/Cocoyam Beans Vegetables Cassava
2	Maize/Cocoyam Beans Vegetables Cassava	Yams Beans Vegetables	Cassava Pigeon peas/ Cucurbits Fallow
3	Cassava Pigeon peas/ Cucurbits Fallow	Maize/Cocoyam Beans Vegetables Cassava	Yams Beans Vegetables
4	Yams Beans Vegetables	Cassava Pigeon peas/ Cucurbits Fallow	Maize/Cocoyam Beans Vegetables Cassava
5	Maize/Cocoyam Beans Vegetables Cassava	Yams Beans Vegetables	Cassava Pigeon peas/ Cucurbits Fallow
6	Cassava Pigeon peas/ Cucurbits Fallow	Maize/Cocoyam Beans Vegetables Cassava	Yams Beans Vegetables

cleared again for further cultivation. Techniques such as dry or leaf mulching and tie or contour ridging are common. Around Maku the slopes are terraced (Fig. 34) but in other areas, notably the Udi escarpment near Enugu and the Awka and Orlu uplands near Onitsha, gully erosion has been very severe (Fig. 35).

In areas where the underlying strata happen to consist of crystalline or volcanic rocks which break down into weathered material rich in plant nutrients, soil fertility may diminish only slowly and may allow continued occupation. If the underlying rocks, however, are sandstones or others containing only small quantities of the substances needed by plants, deterioration may be rapid and recovery very slow indeed. With high precipitation and infiltration, positively charged metallic ions (cations), notably calcium, are leached away, the clays become hydrogen clays and the soils are left acid and unproductive. The secondary forest which re-colonises such areas consists of spindly trees unattractive to the timber merchant and avoided by the cultivator.

The potential productivity of the tropical forest lands for annual crops is limited not only by the fragility of many of the soils but also by the high temperatures and by the even distribution of incoming solar radiation throughout the year. Annual totals of hours of daylight and gross annual photosynthesis are high, but because of

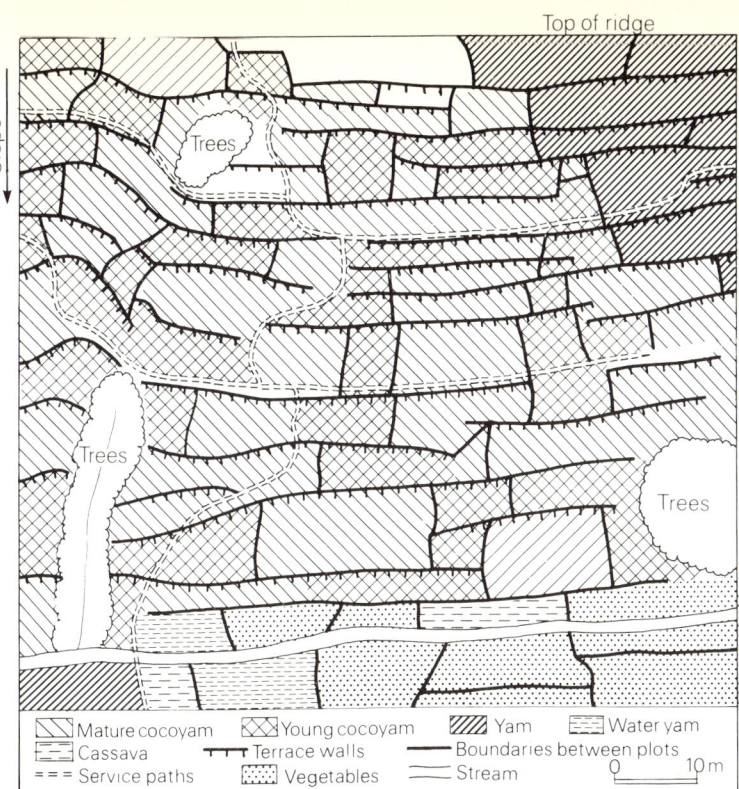

34 Terraced land use around Maku, Nigeria

35 Soil erosion near Onitsha, Nigeria

41

the constantly high temperatures respiration losses are also great so that net primary productivity is only moderate.

Timber

Annual crops like maize and rice have short growing seasons of only four months. In the tropics the number of hours of daylight each day remains about twelve throughout the year, whereas in middle latitudes daylight in the growing season is much longer, about sixteen hours. The highest yields of maize and rice occur in places like California and Spain, in the middle latitudes, where they benefit from the greater amounts of sunlight during the growing season. The humid tropics are more suited to the growth of perennial tree crops which are able to utilise solar energy throughout the year. In addition these crops offer some protection to the soil from the sun and the rain, while their roots draw up nutrients from a depth and their leaves return them to the soil. Large-scale commercial exploitation of the forest lands is, therefore, concerned with the growth of tree crops or the extraction of timber.

Timber extraction is pursued most actively near the coasts where transport costs for this bulky material are low because of the small distances involved. It is a particularly important activity in Gabon, south-western Nigeria, south-west Ghana and the southern Ivory Coast. In the past the exploiters tended to concentrate on a small number of species which had reputations in Europe. This entailed wasting many trees. The value of other species is now recognised and the development of plywood and veneering industries has provided a market for much of the lower-quality wood. Factories like the one that has been established at Sapele in the Niger Delta are amongst the largest manufacturing plants on the continent.

Cocoa in Ghana

The commercial production of cocoa in Ghana was developed by the local people as a small-scale peasant enterprise. These local farmers made use of the introduction of the perennial cocoa tree into west Africa from South America in the late nineteenth century. In the 1890s, farmers from Akwapim (Fig. 36) who had been engaged in the palm-oil trade became interested in the commercial possibilities of the cocoa seedlings which were newly available nearby at the Aburi botanical gardens. As they had insufficient land of their own on which to plant this crop they formed groups in order to purchase surplus land in Akim Abuakwa. The land-use pattern reflects the structure of these land-purchasing organisations. Aburi and Akropong people purchased land as family groups and participants were granted cultivation rights according to their needs, resulting in a mosaic pattern of land-holding and land use (Fig. 37). Krobo people formed companies of unrelated persons to purchase land which was then subdivided into long, narrow, individually owned holdings whose size was based on the contribution of each member to the purchase price. These migrant farmers live on their purchased land or in new towns such as Suhum but they retain strong sentimental links with their ancestral areas. With the profits from the sale of their cocoa they were able to purchase more land further west, as well as build roads and bridges to improve their communications with the ports.

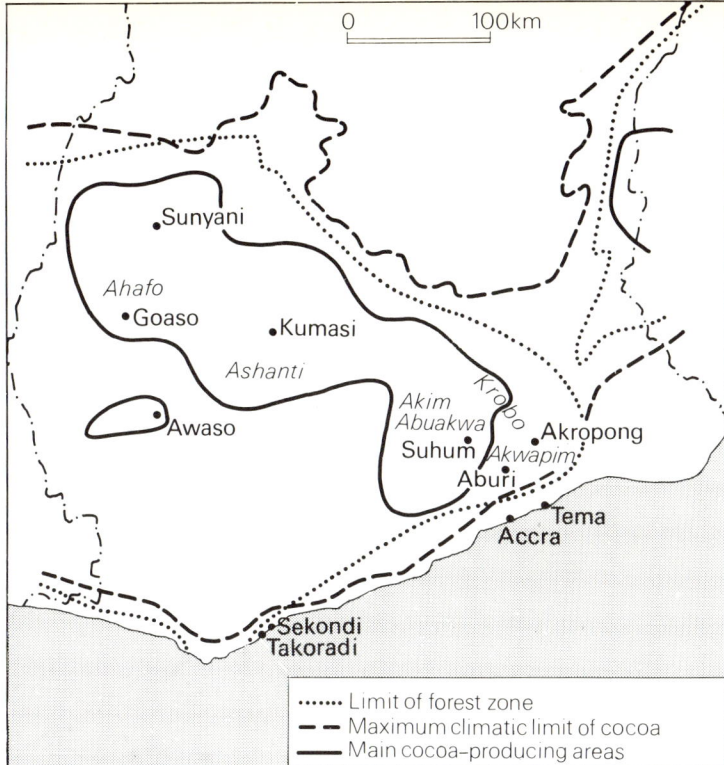

36 Southern Ghana, showing the cocoa-growing areas

37 Patterns of land use among cocoa growers in Ghana
Farm boundaries on land acquired by a. a family group; b. a company

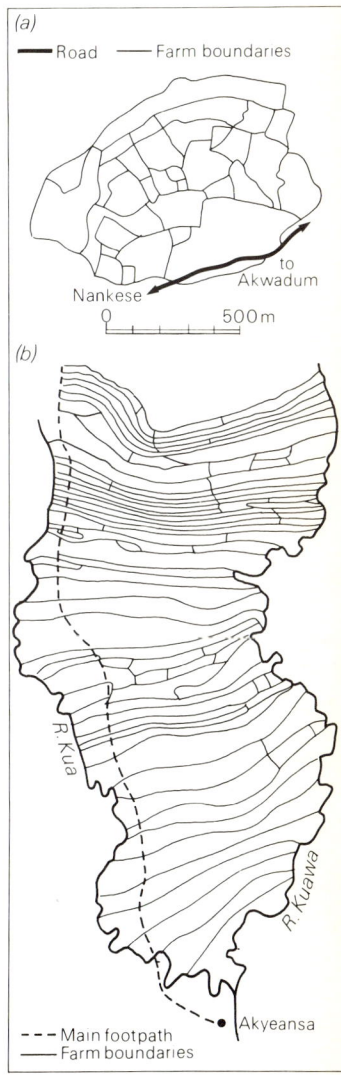

Meanwhile cocoa farming was also taken up by the Akim and Ashanti peoples who planted cocoa on their own family land (Fig. 38). As cocoa grows well only under certain specific conditions of temperature, humidity, soil moisture and fertility (Table 4), the spontaneous spreading of the area under the crop was restricted by physical conditions to certain areas within the forest belt. Cultivation of cocoa involves few inputs from outside the area other than sprays against black pod disease and capsid bugs. The farmers rely mainly on the natural fertility and the fairly well-balanced relationship between their cocoa trees and the soil.

Table 4. Conditions necessary for the successful growth of cocoa

Amount of rainfall	1500 mm to 2000 mm per annum
Rainfall distribution	Rainy season of at least 9 months
Humidity	Constant high humidities, more than 50% all the the year; total annual rainfall should exceed potential evapo-transpiration
Temperature	Mean maximum 30°–32 °C; mean minimum 18°–21 °C
Soil type	Deep red clayey loam; water retentive but well drained
Soil fertility	Newly cleared soil or soil which has been fallow for at least 30 years; pH value 6–7.5; average organic content in top 0–15 cm of soil not less than 3%
Special conditions	Protection from strong winds; shade necessary for young plants
Time to first bearing of fruit	5 years
Years of production	40 years (approximately)
Yields	400 to 560 kg per hectare

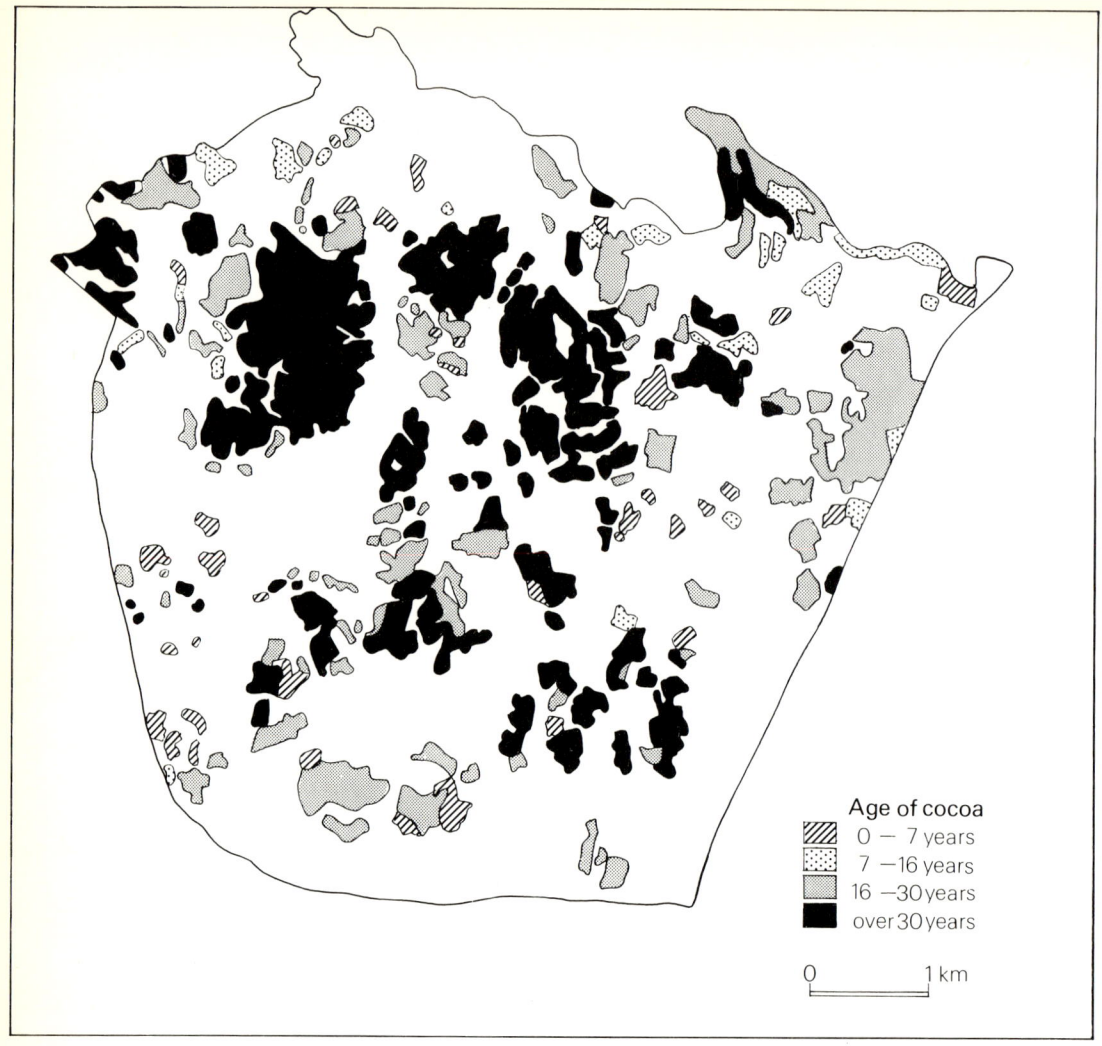

38 Distribution of cocoa trees by age in Akokoaso (Ghana), an Akim village, in 1960

A virus disease called 'swollen shoot', which can be stopped only by cutting out the affected trees, decimated the early Akim cocoa lands and the main areas of cocoa production are now further west, but a project to rehabilitate and replant the cocoa land at Suhum is under way. The young cocoa seedlings require shade during growth and so food crops such as cocoyam and plantain are grown with the seedlings, as cover plants. Once the cocoa trees are established they themselves provide such shade that little grows beneath them. In the cocoa-growing areas food production is frequently insufficient for local needs and more has to be imported from neighbouring areas. Hence cocoa growing has stimulated the growing of food crops for sale in the nearby areas which are unsuitable for growing cocoa. The additional paid labour which is needed for the busy main harvest from September to December often comes from other parts of Ghana and other countries such as Upper Volta, Ivory Coast and Mali. Although the individual scale of production is not large, the cocoa-farming area is generally wealthier than surrounding areas and it has a higher population density and a more elaborate transport network.

Ghana is the leading world producer of cocoa, which provides about half its export earnings. As cocoa trees are a fixed investment

Table 5. Ghana cocoa production and price

Season	Total production, in thousands of long tons	Ghana Producer Price per ton	London Commodity Market Spot Price per ton	
			High	Low
1938–9	298	£ 13	£ 35	£ 20
1948–9	283	121	190	190
1953–4	229	134	562	375
1954–5	242	143	420	254
1955–6	237	149	260	191
1956–7	264	141	360	179
1963–4	436	101	219	178
1964–5	572	92	195	91
1965–6	410	77	225	166
1966–7	376	86	298	214
1967–8	415	103	490	274
1968–9	334	115	472	358
1969–70	404	122	374	264
1970–1	385	122	294	192
1971–2	460	106	348	197
1972–3	410	129	986	317
1973–4	337	159	1255	585
1974–5	376	202	825	540
1975–6	394	222	1482	753

Note: The Ghana Producer Price is the price paid to the producer by the Ghana Cocoa Marketing Board. The London Commodity Market Spot Prices indicate the highest and lowest prices paid for sales of cocoa in London in any one year. (All are rounded figures, and all references are to Imperial tons.)

with an initial time lag before bearing begins, followed by continuous cropping over a generation, it is difficult to vary production in response to market conditions. In the past excessive planting of young trees when world cocoa prices were high has caused over-production at a later date and a consequent drop in the world market prices (Table 5). The cocoa is sold through a marketing board which pays the producer a set price. This can cushion the producers against speculative world price fluctuations but frequently the profits of the marketing board from high world prices are used to subsidise other sections of the country's economy. In terms of purchasing power, the cocoa producers in 1974 received about half what they obtained for their crops in 1951. The cocoa farmers have had difficulty, therefore, in maintaining a high standard of care for their established trees and have planted fewer new trees. Some cocoa is smuggled from Ghana into Togo and the Ivory Coast where purchase prices are higher.

Plantations in Cameroun

Although the major exports of Cameroun are coffee and cocoa, the country provides a contrast with Ghana, for the nineteenth-century German colonists granted land concessions to German companies to establish plantations. They selected the coastal part of West Cameroun where there are fertile volcanic soils on the forested lower

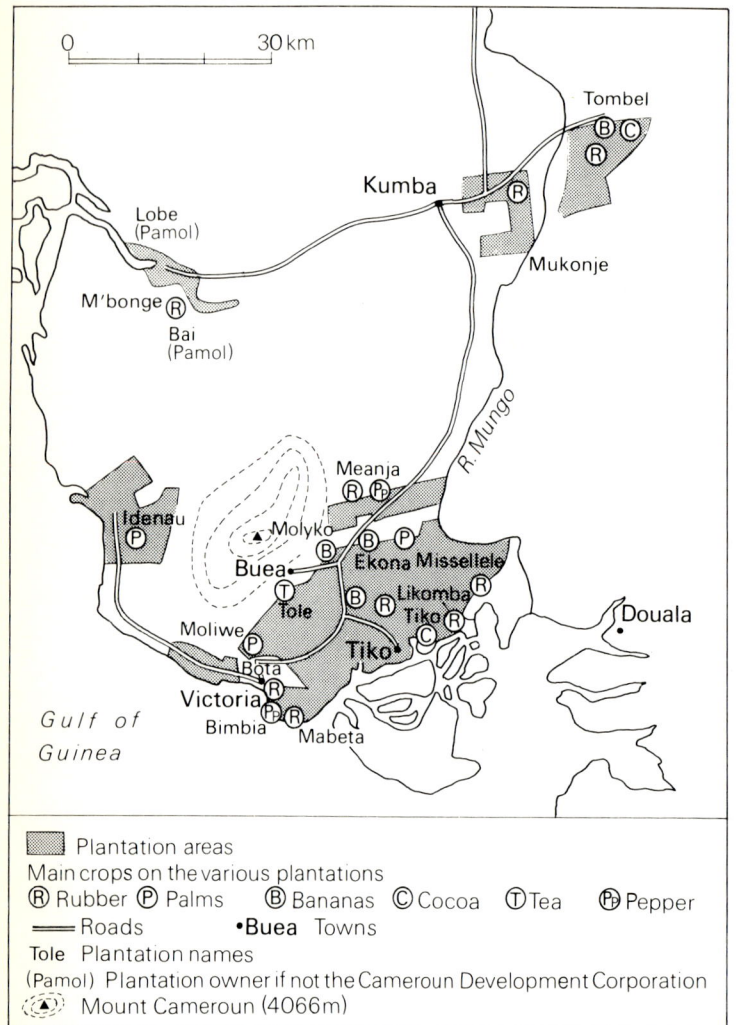

39 Plantations in South West Province, Cameroun

slopes of the Cameroun Mountain and the Tiko Plain, and where conditions were suitable for the establishment of ports such as Victoria and Tiko (Fig. 39). French and British trusteeship replaced the German administration after the 1914–18 War and lasted until the advent of independence in 1960. During this time most of the plantations came to be administered by the Cameroun Development Corporation. The characteristics of these plantations are the concentration on growing tree crops, particularly bananas, *Hevea* rubber and oil palm; the use of a specialised paid labour force; the size and complexity of the organisation; and the frequent association with processing factories or other commercial activities. The Cameroun Development Corporation, for instance, had interests in transport, ports, social services, housing and timber-felling as well as palm oil extraction mills and latex factories. Originally bananas, which are grown widely in tropical Africa by peasant farmers for home consumption, were the most important of the plantation crops here but low prices, world market quotas, problems of wind damage and the incidence of diseases (such as Panama disease) led to a decline in the area under mature banana plants. Peasant cultivation of bananas has proved to be more profitable since greater care in cultivation seems possible with smaller-scale production. Banana plants benefit from manuring and the fruit needs careful handling. The small-scale producers receive advice from the plantation experts and sell their crops through a co-operative union.

The decline in the area of banana production on the plantations has been countered by an increase in the areas planted with rubber trees and oil palms. Job specialisation is found particularly on oil palm plantations, where there are climbers who prune and harvest the palm nuts, specialist nurserymen who look after the young plants, field workers who weed and other workers who load lorries or glean fallen nuts. There has always been a shortage of local people to work on the plantations and most of the labour force comes from other parts of Cameroun or other countries such as Nigeria. Workers stay for limited periods of time but some are encouraged to cultivate small subsistence farms on undeveloped corporation land.

4
The savanna lands

Savanna vegetation covers a more extensive area in Africa than in any other continent, occupying nearly all the huge area between the moist forest and the desert (see Fig. 25, p. 31). The number of trees which grow from 10 to 20 m high varies from place to place; grasses are the most conspicuous plants and may reach heights of 2 m. The rainfall, of between 400 mm and 1400 mm a year, is interrupted by one or two dry seasons when little rain falls and the possible moisture loss from the soil and plants to the air (the potential evapotranspiration) exceeds the supply of water to the soil. Under these conditions seasonal shortage of water sets a limit to crop growth.

Since a much more humid period, lasting from about 12 000 to 4500 years ago in tropical Africa, savanna has encroached on high forest and desert on savanna. Man's activities as a pastoralist and agriculturalist have helped to shift the vegetation zones towards the equator. Without human interference the savanna woodland would probably be denser and grasses would be less conspicuous. Fires caused by lightning are not uncommon, especially at the end of the dry season, but most fires these days are caused deliberately or accidentally by man. Where savanna woodland has been protected from fires and fenced against grazing, the canopy is much more continuous. When trees are cleared at the margins of the high forest, grasses soon begin to colonise the land. If the vegetation is burned annually, to clear the land for cultivation, young trees are prevented from growing so that the boundary between forest and savanna sharpens. Air photographs of the marginal zone show how clear cut are the boundaries between islands of high forest and the wedges of savanna penetrating the forest (Fig. 40).

A few tree species are common to both forest and savanna but generally the combinations of species are quite different. Savanna species are relatively few in number and much more tolerant of fires and drought. Evergreen plants with fleshy leaves are common in the more humid savanna; thorny *Acacias* dominate the drier savanna. Grassland without trees tends to be confined to high plateaus, flood plains and heavy clay soils which dry out and crack in the dry season. In the Sudan Republic, grassy clay plains lie on the east side of the River Nile while the sandy country on the west side, in the same latitude and with the same amount of rainfall, is covered with *Acacia* woodland. Soil contrasts resulting from differing parent materials or different geomorphological histories probably explain the position of the forest–savanna boundary in some areas. Forest persists on deep, porous soils in areas with quite low rainfall totals, while savanna occupies the soils where lateritic ironstone comes close to the surface and impedes root development.

The total bulk of plant material on a unit area of savanna (its

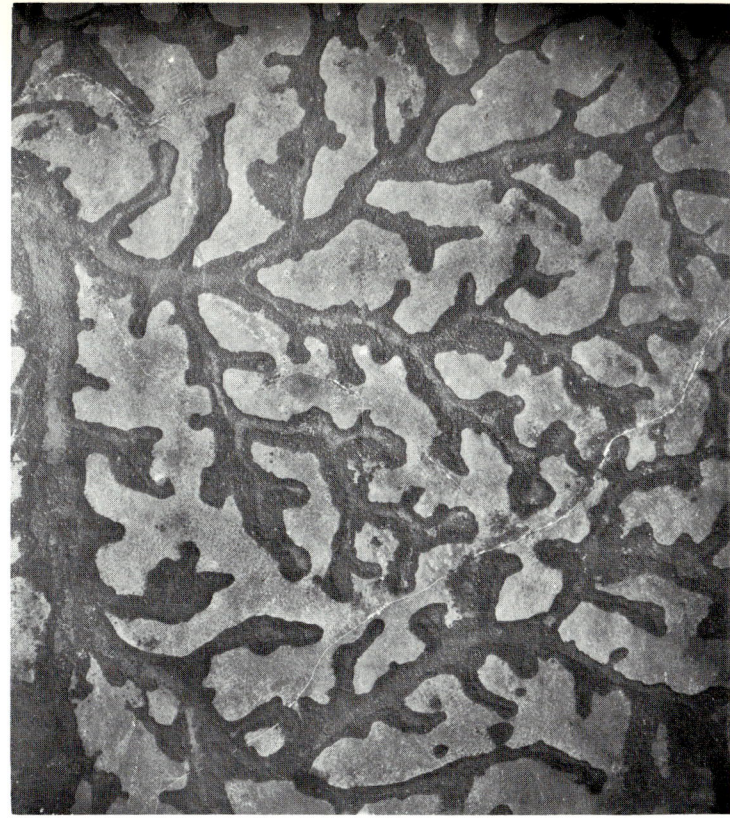

40 An aerial photograph showing the sharp boundaries between forest and savanna vegetation in a riverine area

plant biomass) is much less than that of the same area of forest — something of the order of 40 tonnes per hectare as compared with 450; net productivity is also less. The animal biomass of the savanna is often much greater than that of the forest, especially on the high country of east Africa where there is plenty of surface water for much of the year. The animal biomass consists mainly of ungulates, hoofed mammals including zebra and antelope, together with elephant and, if there are lakes and rivers nearby, hippopotamus. Many of them are ruminants with remarkable digestive systems, capable of breaking down and, in effect, enriching plant material that originally had a low nutritive value. This capacity to make use of low-grade foodstuffs is valuable in the savanna where the nutritive value of the *Andropogon*, *Pennisetum* and *Panicum* genera of grasses rapidly diminishes as they grow tall and the rains come to an end. Many of the animals also browse on trees and are able to make use of the nutrients brought from deep in the soil and incorporated in leaves and seeds.

The animal biomass of the savanna is large. It includes several species of antelope and numerous other big animals which can move long distances quite rapidly, often in large herds. They are able, therefore, to make use of the changing amount and distribution of food and water resources. On the Serengeti Plains of north-western Tanzania, several species of mammal migrate across the plains at different times of the year. First to move through at the end of the dry season is the zebra, which particularly relishes the stems of young grasses. By opening up the herb layer the zebra makes the leaves more accessible for herds of wildebeest. Then comes Thomson's gazelle, which feeds largely on broad-leaved herbs which become available where the other grazing animals have trampled.

Hunters

Man has lived as a hunter in the savanna lands for thousands of years and a good deal is known from archaeological research about his ways of life at different stages. Sites that have been excavated in Africa, especially in the sediments laid down in east African lake basins, have exposed his settlement sites and tools together with the bony remains of his meals.

Hunting peoples are now few in the savanna. Amongst those still in existence are the Hadza of northern Tanzania who live in the country near Lake Eyasi. About 400 of them hunt and gather over an area of about 2500 sq. km. They make use of a wide variety of plants and wild animals and the honey of wild bees. They satisfy their nutritional needs without excessive effort or forethought and without much equipment or organisation. Living in camps of about twenty persons they shift on average about 10 km a fortnight, moving to the vicinity of a large game animal that has been killed or, for example, to avoid evil spirits, considered responsible for runs of misfortune.

The communal life of a hunting people of this kind living in the hill country near the Kenya-Sudan border has been destroyed, however, as a result of agriculturalists encroaching on their hunting territory. The individuals have lost many of the human qualities of caring for close relatives and kindness to those in need, such is the severity of the competition between them for the means to survive at all.

Most rural people in tropical Africa still hunt from time to time and collect honey and fruits, especially in seasons when other food is short. The majority of people in the drier savanna are dependent on their flocks and herds; those of the wetter savanna are primarily cultivators.

Burning vegetation

Whether they are hunters, pastoralists or farmers, savanna people are accustomed to setting fire to the bush and grass at certain times of the year. Hunters light fires to drive game in a required direction, to rocky cliffs or traps where they can readily be killed. Pastoralists seek to encourage a fresh growth of grass with the first rains. Farmers reduce the labour of clearing new plots at the end of the dry season (Fig. 41). Charcoal burners consume the woodland to provide town-dwellers with their fuel. At the end of the dry season, with the grass tall and thoroughly dry, fires are very fierce, killing the fresh shoots of young trees and damaging even the crowns of older ones. Government departments encourage people to burn early in the dry season when fires are less damaging and easier to control, but at the same time sufficiently effective to reduce the risk of fires later in the dry season.

Burning the plant material mineralises some of its components and returns them to the soil, but it also releases large quantities of carbon dioxide, nitrogen compounds and ash into the atmosphere. Smoke from the savanna fires of west Africa merges with finely divided rock debris and tiny shell particles swept up by the wind from dried up lake beds in the southern Sahara, to give the dusty harmattan, the wind that shrouds the Atlantic coast and the savanna lands to the north for days on end between December and March.

41 Savanna vegetation in N. Tanzania felled and burned ready for planting

Pastoralism

Cattle have largely replaced game in the drier savanna areas except in game reserves, most of which are in east Africa. Densities of stocking vary but are about thirty cattle per sq. km over extensive areas. In addition there are usually sheep and goats. Wild mammals may still remain and the human population may number ten or twenty living on the milk from the cattle and goats and locally grown crops. Animal biomass may, therefore, be about 10 or 20 tonnes per sq. km, comparable to that of the wild fauna.

Like the wild game, the domestic herds migrate seasonally. When water and grazing are in short supply at the height of the dry season the herds remain in the vicinity of lakes and flood plains. In the rainy season they move into the drier open country on the watersheds. In this way they take advantage of the grazing and avoid the diseases of the less well drained country at that time of year. Tsetse flies, which carry trypanosomiasis, a disease fatal to cattle and other stock, present the main risk in many regions. Some species of tsetse fly live in particular habitats all the time while others remain in woodland patches in the dry season but spread out over the grassland in the rains (Fig. 42). In parts of the wetter savanna areas of west Africa the pastoralists drive their cattle up to tsetse-free highlands for the rainy season, returning to the plains when the rains cease. The routes followed vary from year to year according to weather conditions and relations with sedentary cultivators, the state governments and taxation authorities.

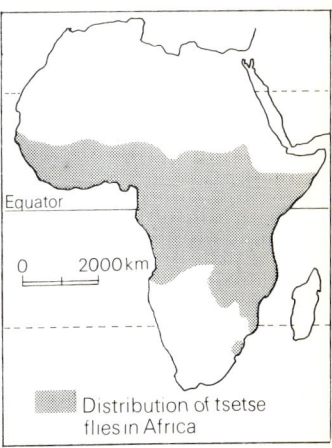

42 The area where tsetse flies are found in Africa

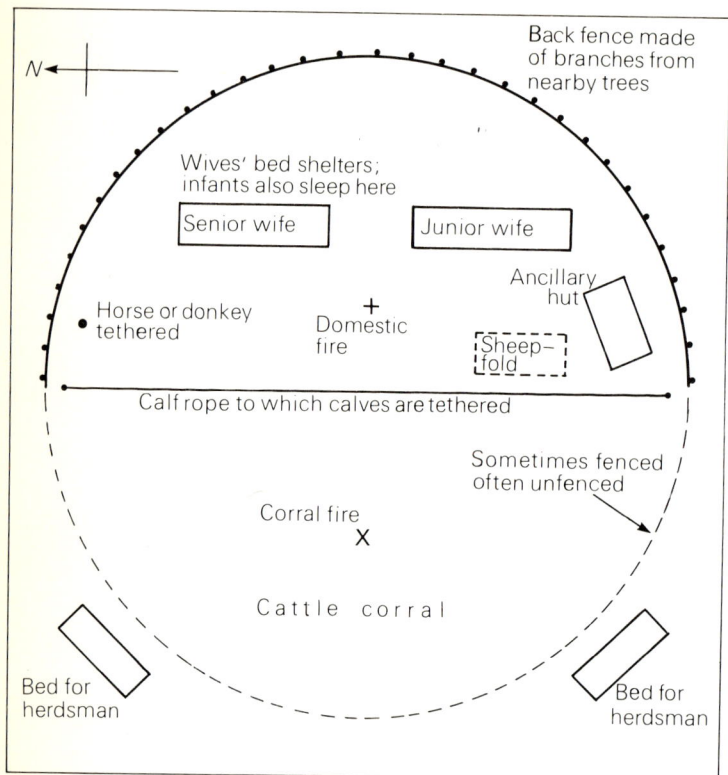

43 Plan of a Fulani homestead

The Fulani
The nomadic Fulani of west Africa, known as Cow or Bush Fulani (Bororo), live on milk. It is the main item of their diet and the aim of every nomadic Fulani family is to have a herd of sufficient size and composition to supply enough milk for all throughout the year. About ten cattle per person are needed to do this. Cattle produce less milk if they do not receive enough food and water, so it is essential to keep them well nourished throughout the year or else the people themselves go hungry.

During the dry season from October to May the herds move towards the more humid south, dispersing in search of pasture and water supplies. They return northwards during the rainy season and concentrate in particular localities. A unit, which consists of about fifteen households and their herds of cattle, sheep and goats, move their homesteads (Fig. 43) over roughly the same restricted circuit year after year until changes in political, economic or ecological conditions cause migrations like the one illustrated in Fig. 44. The nomadic Fulani are reluctant to move into areas they do not know well, since then they would not know where to find good grazing or what the possible hazards are. Grazing in the southern areas is restricted during the wet season both because there is an increased risk of the cattle contracting trypanosomiasis or other diseases and because the sedentary local people use the land then for growing crops. The sedentary cultivators welcome the herds in the dry season since the manure the animals provide improves the fertility of the soil. Normally the nomadic Fulani sell milk, dairy produce

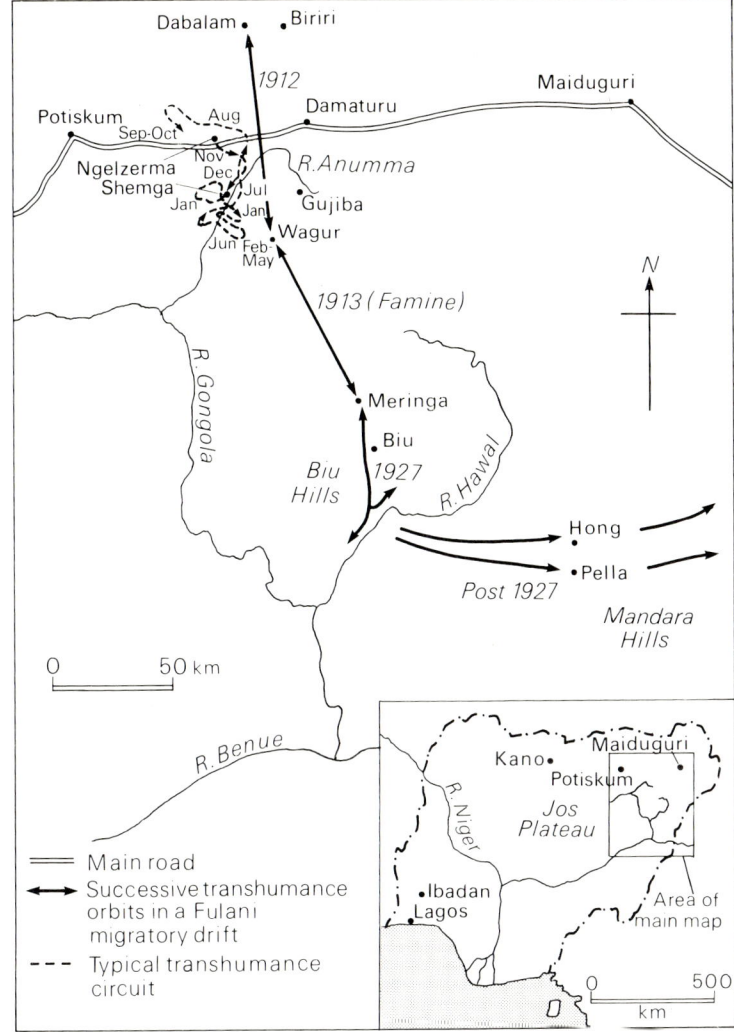

44 A typical transhumance circuit of a group of Fulani pastoralists in Borno State, Nigeria, and a migratory drift in northern Nigeria from 1912 to 1927

and kid leather in order to purchase cereals and to obtain cash to pay the taxes levied on their cattle. There are also a number of poor nomadic Fulani, who have few cattle, and they have to cultivate grain crops in order to survive. Because of their expertise in handling cattle some Fulani are employed as herdsmen for other cattle owners, even as far afield as the Accra Plains of southern Ghana. As payment for their services these herdsmen keep the milk and a proportion of the calves.

The Kanuri
The Kanuri of north-east Nigeria are primarily cultivators but they also keep cattle in their small villages, which are situated on low sandy mounds amid the clay plains near Lake Chad. The herds from some of the villages are traditionally moved each dry season to distant pastures, but the majority remain based in their villages to which they return each evening. The cattle are taken out to graze each day. They are capable of travelling about 14 km a day and

53

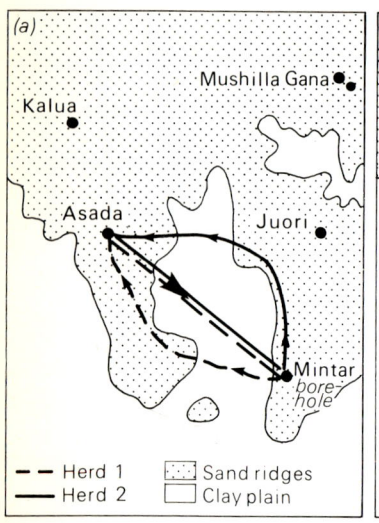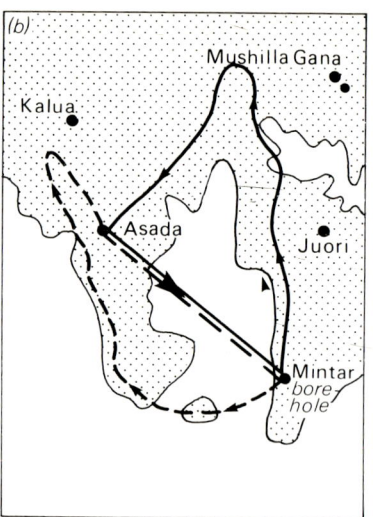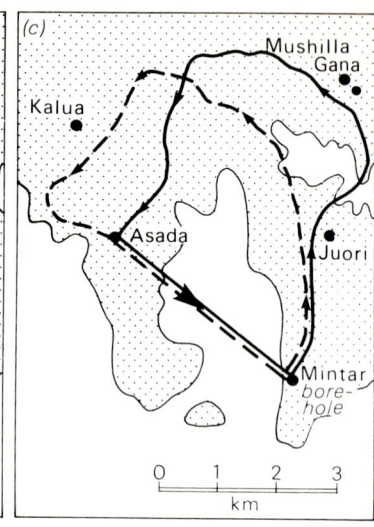

45 Water/grazing circuits from a Kanuri village in northern Nigeria
The clay plain is barren: grazing is confined to the sandy areas. Each day both herds set out from Asada village, water at Mintar borehole and slowly return to the village, grazing as they go. The lengths of their circuits are kept to a minimum and do not normally exceed 18 km. As the dry season advances the grazing circuits get longer as the herds seek grass further afield. a. The circuit on 3 November 1972 (early dry season); b. on 24 and 25 February 1973 (mid-dry season); c. on 1 and 2 June 1973 (end of dry season)

follow a circuit. This depends on the source of water and the distribution of pasture, which is largely confined to the sandy areas. Where the well or borehole is situated in a village the possible grazing area is a circle centred on the village with a radius of 7 km. Where the watering point is at a distance from the village the potential grazing area forms an ellipse with the village and the well at the two foci. The grazing areas of different villages overlap but it is possible to calculate the pressure on the pastures and to see how the villagers adjust their grazing strategies to the situation as it fluctuates from season to season and year to year (Fig. 45).

Cultivation

Wide areas of the upland savanna plains have poor soils derived from ancient weathered parent material, low in plant nutrients. Cultivation is unrewarding on any one plot of land for more than a few years and then the soil has to be rested in some cases for several decades. The biomass of the open woodland and its store of nutrients is fairly small.

The Bemba

On the upland plains of Zambia, for example, the Bemba people concentrate the accumulated nutrients of a wide area, about 2.4 hectares of woodland, onto a smaller plot of about 0.4 hectares. The branches of the trees on the big plot are cut down during the dry season and dragged to a main central area where they are formed into a stack about half a metre high which is then burned (Fig. 46). Clearing the savanna vegetation is less arduous than cutting down tropical forest but a larger acreage of land for cultivation is required so the total work involved may be more than in the forest. Burning the accumulated debris clears the ground of low vegetation and makes the surface soil more friable, while the resulting ash adds some potassium and other nutrients. When the rains come, finger millet (*Eleusine* spp.), which is the staple crop, and *Sorghum* and maize are sown broadcast over the plot, and gourds (*Lagenaria* spp.) and marrows (*Cucurbita* spp.) are planted round the edge. After this

46 Calendar of seasonal activities among the Bemba

Month		Jan	Feb	Mar	Apr	May	June	July	Aug	Sept	Oct	Nov	Dec
	Weather	Heavy rain	Rain slackening	Rains cease		C o l d			H o t			Early rains	Mid rains
	Food supply	Hunger months	Subsidiary crops Cucurbits ripe	ripe	Early millet ripe	A m p l e	f o o d	s u p p l y			Less food	Getting scarce	Hunger month
Men's work	Millet farms, etc.		Fencing farms				T r e e	c u t t i n g			Firing farms		Sowing main crop
	Subsidiary crops	Mound digging and sowing							Dry-weather sowing			Mound digging and sowing	
	Other activities	Setting fishing traps and nets	Building houses (new village)		Setting fish weirs				Fish poisoning Net hunting			Fish spearing and trapping on flats	
Women's work	Farms			H a r v e s t i n g: maize	early millet	main crop millet			Piling branches		Firing farms		Sowing main crop
	Gardens	Mound digging and sowing					Harvesting groundnuts		Dry-weather sowing			Mound digging and sowing	
	Other activities	Collecting mushrooms and caterpillars		Collecting caterpillars					Collecting wild spinaches Fish poisoning			Fruits	Collecting mushrooms

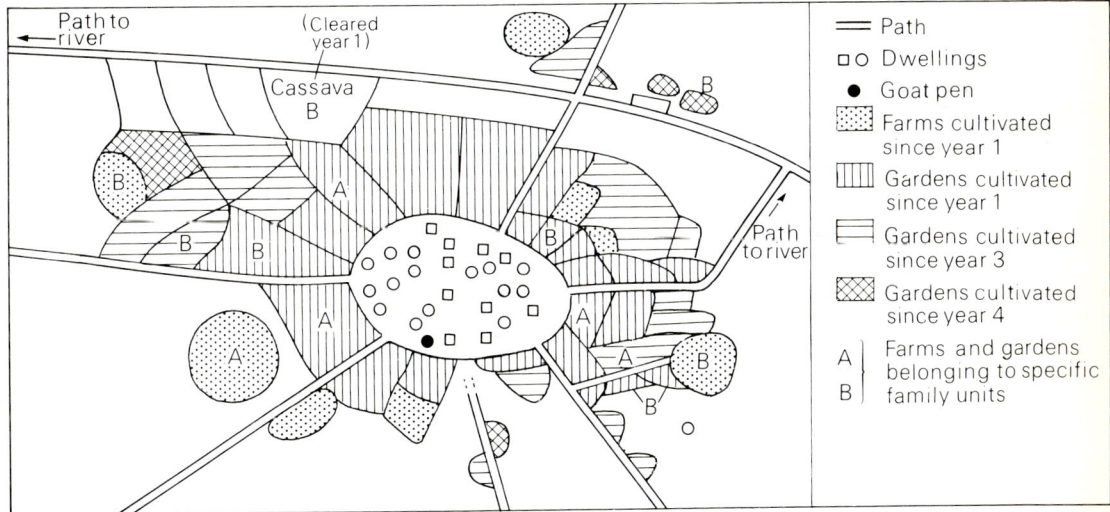

47 Plan of a Bemba village in Zambia and associated land use in the fifth year of occupation

initial grain crop, groundnuts can be grown successfully on the plot in the following year. As time goes on the soil fertility declines, weeds begin to proliferate and the plots are eventually abandoned. In the meantime new plots are cleared ready for cultivation (Fig. 47).

Around their small dispersed villages the Bemba also create gardens where they grow a wide variety of crops such as maize, gourds, cow peas (*Vigna unguiculata*), cassava, tobacco and sweet potatoes. Refuse and manure are added to the garden soil, which is

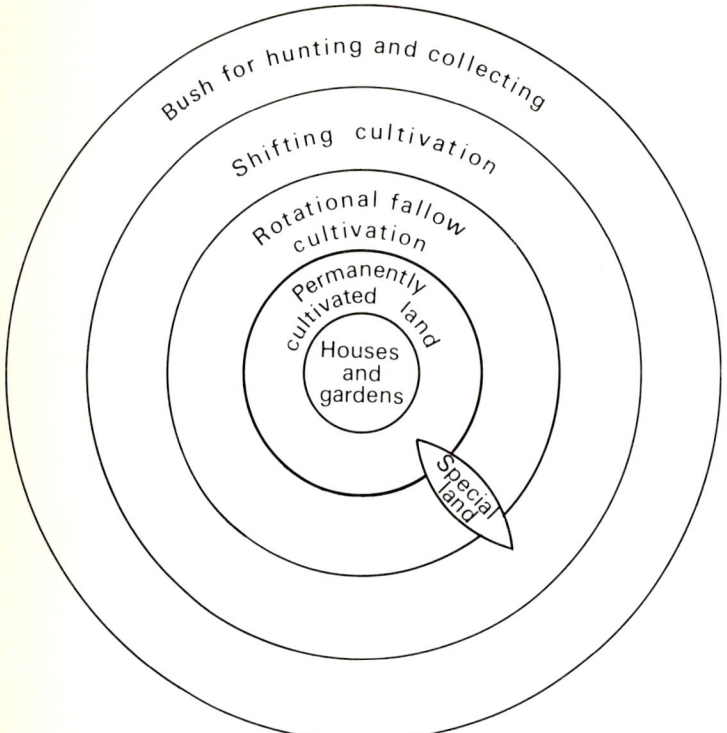

48 Diagram of land zoning common in the savanna areas of tropical Africa 'Special land' includes valley bottom land where swamp rice, sugar cane and sweet potatoes can be grown or particular soil conditions are favourable for specific crops

heaped up into mounds to improve its drainage, aeration and structure. The sites of former dwellings are particularly valued as gardens and are planted with crops for many years.

As farm plots are cleared further and further from the village every year, the people find that they may have to walk up to 16 km to reach them. At this point they may decide to move the village to a new site where fields can be cleared close to the settlement. When the fields are at a great distance from the village, the Bemba build temporary huts on the plots to live in when they are working there. This Bemba system of shifting cultivation, often called the *chitimene* system, is on the decline now, for many of the men have left their villages to go to work in the mines of the Copper Belt. Without the assistance of the men, the women find it difficult to clear the main farm plots and many Bemba have moved their villages to sites near the main roads where alternative ways of making a living exist, such as selling prepared food to travellers.

Under conditions of low population density, shifting cultivation is an efficient system. The farmers make careful use of the variety of environmental conditions and allow sufficient fallow time for the regeneration of lost nutrient material. The system, however, is unable to absorb more than a limited population growth without resulting in a decline in farming standards. Most measures to increase the area under cultivation or the yields per hectare lead to shorter fallow periods and make re-growth of natural vegetation and the restoration of fertility more difficult.

In the savanna areas the rotational fallow type of cultivation is

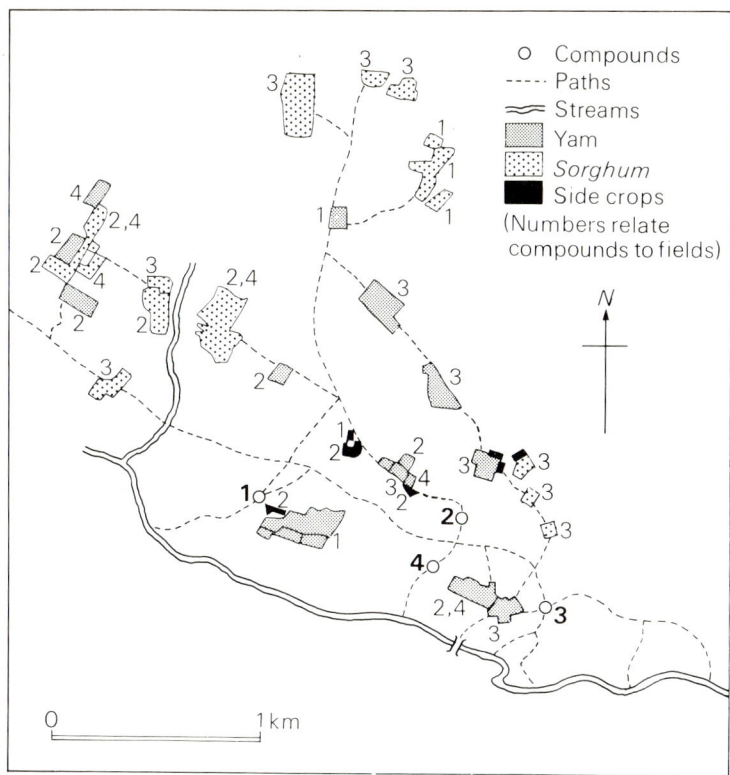

49 Lands and compounds of MbaAliko in northern Tivland, Nigeria

very well developed. The land-use pattern, particularly in west Africa, often displays a concentric arrangement, the intensity of farming decreasing with increasing distance from the homestead or village (Fig. 48). Although all three systems of cultivation we are discussing appear in this pattern, the largest area and the one most important for production is that under rotational fallow cultivation.

The Tiv
The Tiv people occupy a large area of Nigeria, mainly south of the River Benue but north of the forest zone. The density of population in their area increases from 10 persons per sq. km in the north to 200 persons per sq. km in the south west. The Tiv, typically, live in oval compounds separated from one another by tens or hundreds of metres but linked together by an intricate system of paths (Fig. 49). All Tiv belong to family groups who trace their descent from a common ancestor. There is no central authority and family groups often expand their own land areas by claiming land from the particular family group with land adjacent to theirs but to whom they are most distantly related. In this way the Tiv have migrated northwards across Tivland, frequently quarrelling quite violently over land ownership.

Although land belongs to the family group, cultivation is an individual rather than a group activity. Tobacco, cotton, indigo (*Indigofera* spp.), green vegetables and fruits are grown beside the compounds, and cattle may be tethered there during the day. Beyond this area lies the main cropland where yams and other crops are

Table 6. Variations in Tiv agriculture

	Location		
	S. Tivland MbaGor	S. Tivland Iyon	N. Tivland MbaAliko
Population	477	1047	167
Density of pop. per sq. km	103	213	25
Total area in hectares	458.0	486.8	c. 680.0
Area under cultivation in hectares	131.1	170.4	50.1
% of land under cultivation	28	35	7
No. of cultivated hectares per person	0.27	0.17	0.30
Hectares of yams	60.9	65.4	23.0
Hectares of yams per person	0.13	0.06	0.14
% of area under yams	46.5	38.4	46.0
% of area under millet and *Sorghum*	30.3	29.9	51.0
% of area under beniseed	10.0	17.5	–
% of area under cassava	3.1	4.4	–
% of area under fallow crops	10.1	9.8	3.0

grown on mounds. A plot is cultivated for about three years and then allowed to lie fallow for up to sixteen years in some areas. In places where the population densities are high the land is carefully cleared of even the stumps of trees, creating a landscape of cultivated land dotted with occasional useful trees. In pockets of swampy land several crops of quick-maturing maize or one irrigated crop of swamp rice are grown. Although there is a wide variation in the size of farms, the percentage of land under cultivation at any one time increases with increasing population densities but the average field size diminishes as the density of population increases. Where population densities are high, fewer yams are grown, being replaced by more cassava and beniseed (*Sesamum indicum*) (Table 6). Some yams are exported but the main commercial crop is beniseed. There are few urban areas in Tivland but markets are a very important feature of Tiv life (they are discussed further in Chapter 7).

The Sukuma
The Sukuma live in the drier savanna areas of Tanzania, close to Lake Victoria. The rainfall is about 700 mm per year and the rainy season lasts about six months. It includes a period of short rains in October and a period of longer rains in March. The various governments of Tanzania have encouraged the Sukuma to grow cotton as a cash crop. The increase in the planting of cotton meant that less land was available for food crops, and the people changed from a system of shifting cultivation to rotational fallow cultivation. Although the area planted with cotton has increased greatly, little attention has been paid to soil conservation methods or ways of increasing yields.

There are a number of different soil types on the rolling hills of Sukumaland. The variations in soil depend on its position in relation

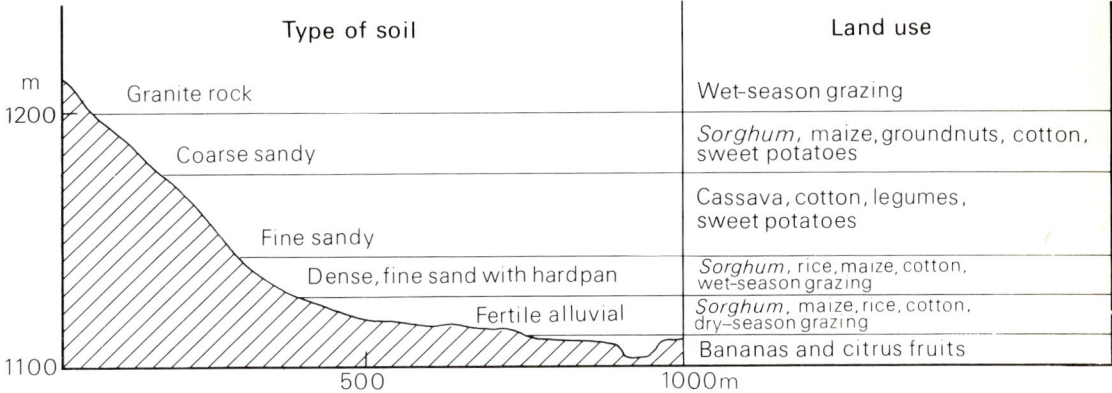

50 A Sukuma land-holding at Nyashishi, Tanzania, demonstrating the principal uses of different types of soil

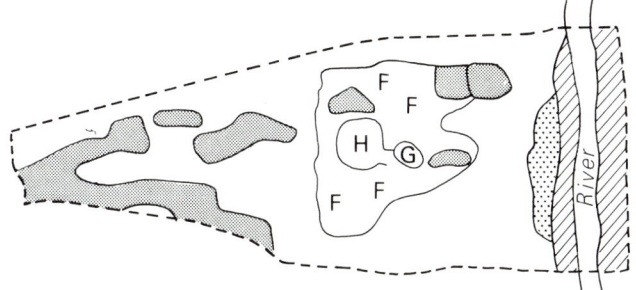
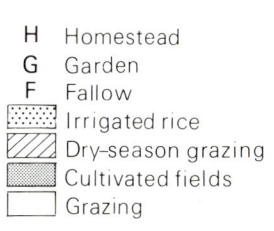

to the slope. The Sukuma farmers have taken advantage of this and a typical farm is a strip of land stretching from the top of a hill to the bottom (Fig. 50). In this way they are able to include in their farms riverside grazing for animals in the dry season, hilltop grazing for animals in the wet season and, in between, soils which will support different crops. The Sukuma combine cultivation with animal husbandry but do not integrate the two. This means that animal manure is not used systematically on the fields, nor are fodder crops grown to feed the animals. They graze on pasture and fallow land which is open to all; the farmers have proprietory rights only over land under cultivation. Cattle are a sign of wealth and prestige and the main source of animal protein in the Sukuma diet. By keeping a large number of cattle a farmer can take most advantage of the communal pastures. Overgrazing and erosion have resulted from this practice but more cattle continue to be bought with the money obtained from the sale of cotton, which is planted on about half a farmer's cultivated land each year. The remaining land is hoed into ridges, which improves both the soil structure and its capacity to absorb water. The ridges are planted with subsistence crops such as maize, cassava and beans (*Phaseolus vulgaris*). Planting takes place over a considerable period, thus spreading the work load and ensuring a fresh food supply for a long period each year. As in so many other areas, rice and sweet potatoes are grown on especially moist plots in the valley bottoms. There do not seem to be any important crop sequences in Sukumaland. Plots are planted with the crop that thrives best on them until the yields decline or the weeds

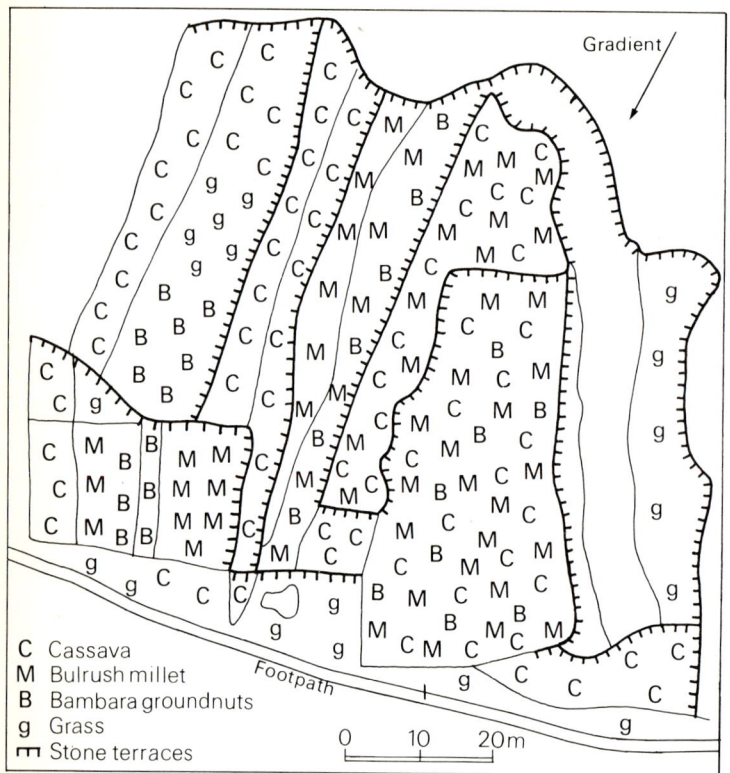

51 A Kara farm in Tanzania, showing the terraces

become too persistent. Cassava, however, is often the final crop before the land is left to revert to a grass fallow. About seven years of fallow follow seven years of cultivation. Sisal (*Agave sisalana*) hedges are planted as boundaries to fields and the leaves are sold for fibre.

The Kara
The soil on the island of Ukara within the Tanzanian part of Lake Victoria is composed of weathered granite and is not very fertile. Despite this the Kara people on the island number more than 200 persons per sq. km. Only by cultivating the land intensively and permanently can the Kara hope to make a living. Some have emigrated to the neighbouring island of Ukerewe and the Tanzanian mainland where they practise rotational fallow cultivation. Seasonal and short-term migrations from the island are now also common. Nearly all the island is used in some way for farming. Each family, which includes about ten persons, cultivates two hectares of land and has one hectare of grazing land in the upland area. Some of the grazing in the centre of the island is communally owned but in general land is individually owned. Fertiliser is essential to keep the land under cultivation year after year and so each family has a few animals, usually about two cows and two sheep or goats. Fodder and pasture are restricted and the number of animals has to be limited, but cattle are not a sign of wealth and prestige as they are in neighbouring Sukumaland. They are valued more for the manure they provide than for their meat. Fish from the lake are the main

source of protein. The cattle are kept in stone-lined stalls which conserve as much as possible of the manure. Fodder grasses from the centre of the island and numerous other leaves and crop residues are fed to the cattle. About ten tonnes of manure are spread on a hectare of ground each year.

As well as this the Kara grow leguminous crops such as *Crotolaria striata*, which is dug into the soil after about nine months of growth. These green manure crops both enrich the soil and protect it from erosion during their growth. Erosion is a continuing problem. The Kara have developed techniques of terracing and ridging on the arable land (Fig. 51) but the grazing land is not similarly protected. On unirrigated land cultivation follows a three-year rotation (Table 7). The fields in the bottoms of valleys and beside Lake Victoria are irrigated. Ditches and trenches are excavated and the soil dug out is used to improve other plots. The Kara grow rice on their irrigated plots and between the rice harvest and the next rice planting they cultivate sweet potatoes, vegetables and *Sorghum* (Fig. 52). Although they work very hard and their returns per hectare are about three times greater than those in neighbouring areas they do not grow many cash crops. They place more emphasis on better food than on the acquisition of more consumer goods.

Table 7. The Kara three-year rotation

Year 1	August	Manure applied
	September/October	Bulrush millet planted; *Crotolaria striata* planted when bulrush millet 30 cm high
	January/February	Bulrush millet harvested
	March/June	*Crotolaria* grows to 120–50 cm high
Year 2	July	*Crotolaria* dug in as green manure
	September/October	A self-seeded crop of bulrush millet begins to grow
	November/January	Bambara nuts (*Voandzeia subterranea*) or groundnuts planted between growing bulrush millet plants
	January/February	Bulrush millet harvested
	June	Bambara nuts or groundnuts harvested
Year 3	July/September	Manure applied
	September/October	A self-seeded crop of bulrush millet begins to grow
	January/February	Bulrush millet harvested
	February/April	*Sorghum* sown or planted
	June	*Sorghum* harvested

The Hausa

One of the most extensive areas of permanently cultivated land in tropical Africa is in Hausaland in northern Nigeria. The most heavily settled area is around the city of Kano, where most of the land is cropped every year. The population density and the proportion of permanently cultivated land decreases with increasing distance from the city. The main staple crops here are *Sorghum*, millet and cow peas while the groundnuts are both the main cash crop and a local food crop.

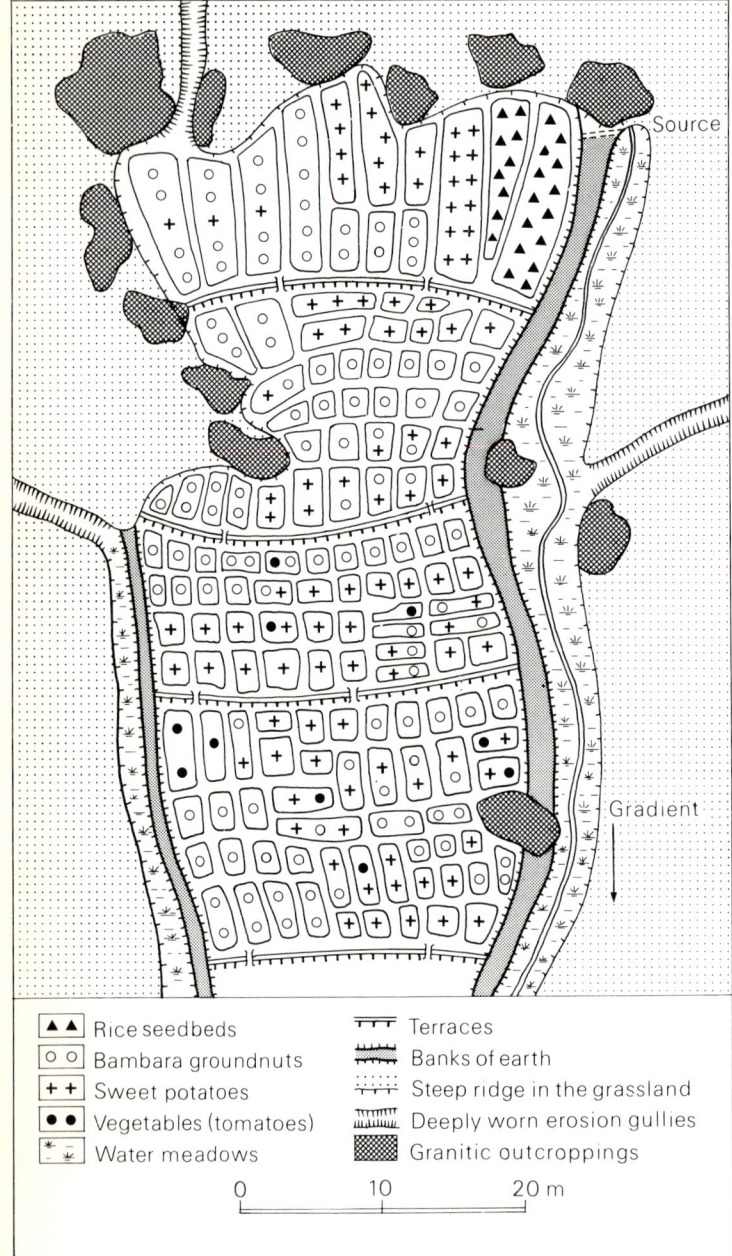

52 An example of irrigation farming in winter on Ukara Island, Tanzania
In summer almost all of the plots grow rice

▲▲ Rice seedbeds
○○ Bambara groundnuts
++ Sweet potatoes
●● Vegetables (tomatoes)
*⚹ Water meadows
⊤⊤⊤ Terraces
Banks of earth
Steep ridge in the grassland
Deeply worn erosion gullies
Granitic outcroppings

0 10 20 m

Fertility, which is not naturally very high, is maintained by various means. Within a few miles of Kano city, waste from the slaughter houses, refuse dumps and latrines is applied to the fields. At greater distances from the city, manure for the fields comes from the cattle, sheep and goats which graze the impoverished grasslands and stubble fields in the dry season, but are kept in stalls in the villages during the wet season when the crops are growing. Nomadic Fulani are encouraged to graze their herds on the stubble fields

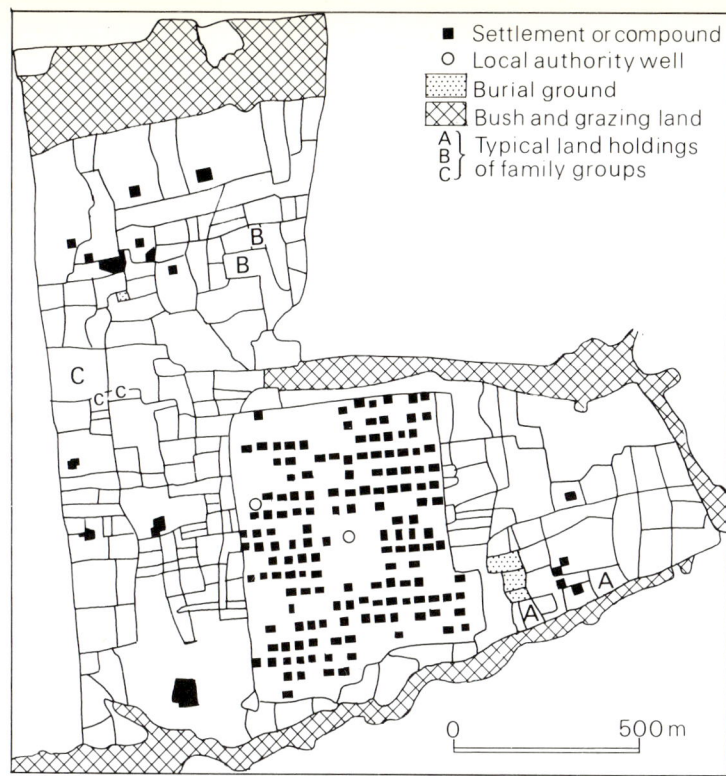

53 Land use around Sabon Birni in northern Nigeria

54 A shaduf irrigating a vegetable garden beside a dry river bed near Kano, Nigeria

55 A typical dry-season crop pattern on a *fadama* farm

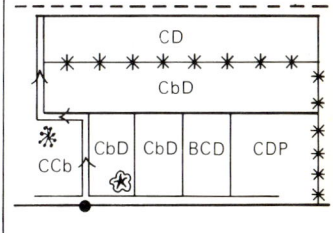

during the dry season. The fields are generally rectangular and are protected from domestic animals by hedges of grasses, shrubs or cacti (Fig. 53). In the fields the crops are grown in various associations on ridges and weeding is done with care. Seasonally flooded areas or land close to permanent water courses, which can be irrigated by shaduf-fed channels, is known as *fadama* land (Figs. 54, 55). This land is normally cultivated in the dry season when the other fields lie fallow and some valuable crops of vegetables, particularly onions (*Allium cepa*) and peppers (*Capsicum* spp.), sugar-cane, maize and rice are grown there.

The Ewe
A further example of permanent cultivation is found in the dry coastal zone of south-east Ghana, where the Ewe of the Volta Delta construct raised beds of soil. Here they grow a variety of crops with the aid of fish, bat and cattle manure, incorporating crop residues in the soil and hauling up water in buckets from wells which tap freshwater aquifers at a shallow depth in the coastal sandbars fronting the delta. Shallots (*Allium ascalonicum* – small onions) are the most valuable crop grown. Lorry loads worth hundreds of thousands of pounds annually are carried to Accra.

Permanent cultivation without the use of artificial fertilisers is possible in some areas of tropical Africa within the context of the traditional land-use systems. It entails making the maximum use of all the opportunities offered by the local environment, which in turn requires the development of appropriate techniques. Not all the areas of permanent cultivation are especially favourable for agriculture but population densities in these areas are invariably high. In some instances the ability to cultivate land year after year is at the expense of other land which contributes to the fertility of the cultivated land but becomes impoverished and eroded in the process.

Modernisation of farming

Modern technology has enabled the farmers in some areas to make use of nutrient substances, energy and water derived from sources well outside their immediate vicinity. Artificial fertilisers are applied to cash crops such as groundnuts thereby replacing, at rather high cost, the phosphorus and nitrogen being exported in the form of nuts, oil and cattle cake. Pesticides are not widely used as yet and tractors have not made much impact outside the main areas of European settlement. One exception is the Gedaref area of the eastern Sudan Republic where tractors were introduced in the late 1940s to disc-harrow the land in preparation for sowing; here large areas are under mechanised cultivation.

Mechanised irrigation schemes are in operation in many countries but the areas involved are fairly small. European settlement in countries such as Rhodesia and Kenya heralded the introduction of new farming methods on a large scale. In other countries the governments have encouraged the adoption of different methods, with varying degrees of success.

Kenyan agriculture
About two-thirds of Kenya is agriculturally unproductive because of the unreliable rainfall (see Fig. 6) and so about 95% of the population live in one-third of the country. Following the construction of the Uganda railway, which reached Lake Victoria in 1902, many Europeans settled in Kenya. From Nairobi to the Uganda border the railway passes through well-watered fertile hilly country over 1500 m above sea level, where the climate is pleasant for Europeans despite the equatorial latitudes. These 'White Highlands', as they were called, were not regarded as belonging to the local Africans and until 1961 were reserved by the government for European occupation. The Europeans used to run (and some still do) large mechanised commercial farms employing much African labour. There are three main types of farming, depending on the local physical conditions: tea

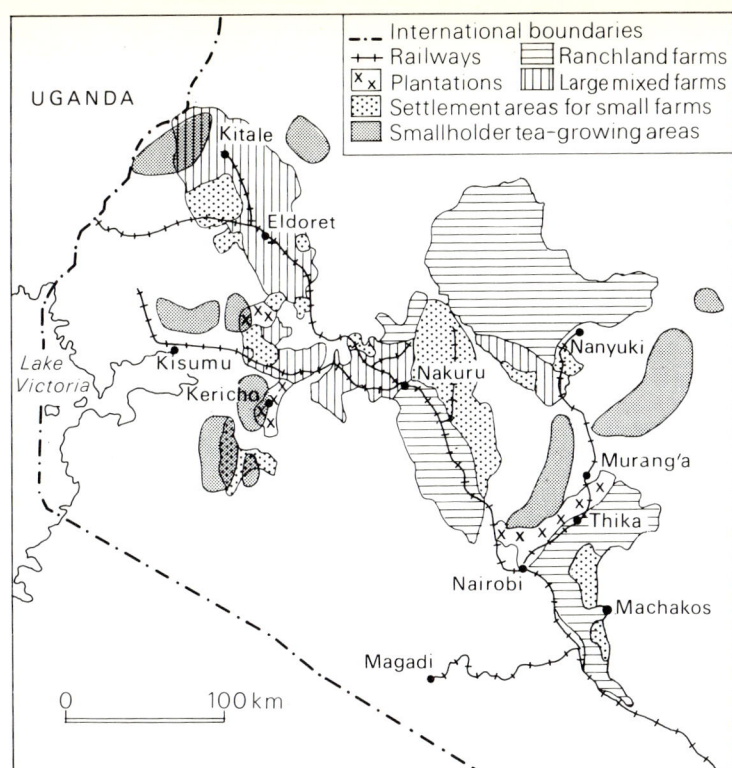

56 The farming pattern in the highland area of Kenya

(*Camellia sinensis*) and coffee plantations around Kericho and Nairobi; beef cattle and sheep in the drier areas; and mixed farming in the wetter areas where the main products include maize, pyrethrum (*Chrysanthemum cinerariifolium*) wheat (*Triticum* spp.), sisal, dairy cattle, sheep, pigs and poultry (Fig. 56). In 1960 most of Kenya's four leading agricultural exports came from these 'White Highlands' (Table 8), where the transport network was most developed. Considerable changes have taken place since then.

Table 8. Principal agricultural exports from Kenya in 1960 compared with 1974

	Coffee	Tea	Sisal	Pyrethrum
1960				
% of total value of exports	29.2	12.5	13.0	8.6
Total production in thousands of tonnes	31.6	13.8	63.6	8.6
European-owned farm production, in thousands of tonnes	25.6	13.7	60.6	6.8
European-owned farm production as % of total production	81.0	99.3	95.2	78.8
1974				
% of total value of exports	23.6	11.9	10.4	2.8
Total production in thousands of tonnes	70.1	53.4	86.5	14.4
Smallholder production, in thousands of tonnes	39.3	n.a.	n.a.	12.5
Smallholder production as % of total production	56.1	n.a.	n.a.	87.0

n.a. = figures not available

57 Traditional Kikuyu land use near Murang'a (Fort Hall), Kenya in 1902

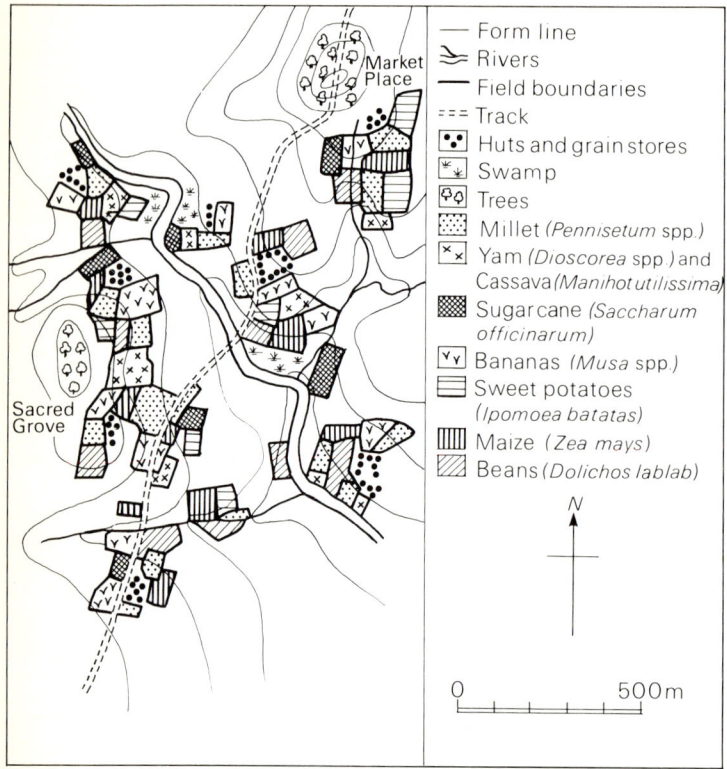

The Mau Mau rebellion of the 1950s, provoked by the overcrowded conditions in the Kikuyu reserves, resulted in the enforced movement of these dispersed people into compact villages. Later, with the Kikuyus' consent, the fragmented traditional Kikuyu farms (Fig. 57) growing millet and maize were consolidated into single units and enclosed. Farmers were given individual legal titles to these enclosed farms, which were comparable in area with all their previous holdings (Fig. 58). Loans, assistance with soil conservation measures and help in planning the farms to grow both subsistence and cash crops were made available (Fig. 59). Mixed farming now predominates with cash crops such as *arabica* coffee (the best-quality coffee, which is a native of Ethiopia and grows best at an altitude between 600 and 750 m), pyrethrum, maize and dairy cattle. Crop zoning occurs according to the altitude and rainfall, while the development of a zone of dairy farming and market gardening around Nairobi indicates a demand for these products rather than particular ecological conditions.

Land consolidation, the granting of legal titles and an increasing population left some people in Kenya without any land. To overcome this problem the government purchased the farms of Europeans who left the country when it became independent in 1963. These have been fragmented and sold to African settlers with the result that, on the completion of the scheme in 1970, some 1000 large European farms on 494 000 hectares of land had been replaced by 34 000 small African farms. Subdivision of farms ceased to be government policy in 1971. The new settlement policy known as the *shirika*

59 The land holdings on this hillside near Nyeri, Kenya, have been consolidated and are now used in an orderly manner. Grazing land on the lower slopes is protected from erosion by contour terracing. Behind and to the right of the round houses and grain stores are bananas and maize and vegetables

58 Contrasting patterns of Kikuyu land-holdings; a. before and b. after consolidation. Shading indicates holdings of one landowner

programme takes over large farms as a unit and runs them on a commercial basis. *Shirika* members are allocated a subsistence plot of about one hectare and work for a regular wage on the main farm under experienced management. Other people have become tenant farmers on schemes like the Mwea Irrigation Settlement where they grow rice. Commercial agricultural produce now comes from both large and small farms and there have been widespread increases in output since 1966. Small-scale tea production (see Fig. 56) has been particularly successful, with a fourfold increase in growers and a sixfold increase in planted area between 1964 and 1974, while the export value of fresh fruit and vegetables increased sixfold between 1968 and 1973. Marketing boards and co-operative societies play an important part in maintaining standards and stabilising earnings. Kenya is now planning to develop the remaining two-thirds of the country, which receives less than 500 mm rainfall per annum, for beef production and game parks, but the well-watered highlands and the lowlands near Lake Victoria continue to provide the basis for economic development.

5
The arid lands

Most of tropical Africa north of a line from the mouth of the Senegal River to northern Ethiopia is desert (Fig. 60), as is the Namib coast in the south-west of the continent (see Fig. 25, p. 31). Somalia, much of Kenya and the Kalahari are so dry that, although they are plant-covered, agriculture without irrigation is scarcely possible. Conditions range from the hyper-arid central Sahara, where there may be no living thing in sight, to the wooded steppe with 400 mm of rain per annum on average, supporting large herds of game or domestic animals. In all these arid areas plant productivity is limited by shortage of water and the stability of the ecosystem is easily upset by human interference, drought or sequences of dry years.

The great extent of deserts and the degree of dryness have existed in tropical Africa for only about 5000 years. Before that time, for 5000 years or more, lakes had been more extensive and precipitation

60 Veiled Touareg riding into Timbuktu This famous old town, a little way north of the Niger in Mali, is in the Sahel, but heavy grazing and trampling over the area within a few kilometres has reduced it to desert

greater than at present by 50% or more. About 17 000 years ago, at the height of the last glacial period in Europe and North America, on the other hand, temperatures were several degrees lower between the tropics and precipitation was also less than it is now. Desert dunes extended towards the equator, occupying great tracts of alluvial basins that today receive as much as 400 mm or even 1000 mm of rain annually. In the wetter period that followed, the dunes were colonised by grasses and trees and today open woodland persists over much of the Sahel on the southern fringe of the Sahara and over the sands which were shaped by the wind in western Rhodesia and Botswana, bordering and within the Kalahari.

Desert conditions have persisted in some parts of Africa for thousands, possibly millions, of years. Many plants and animals are adapted in their morphology, physiology and behaviour to the stresses of desert life. Over half the desert plants are short-lived herbs that can complete their life cycles within a couple of months, when rain is sufficient to cause germination of the seeds. Many of the perennial plants are succulents able to accumulate and store water. The stomata (pores) of cacti close during the day, when evaporation stress is high, and open at night. The non-succulents have very extensive root systems with about 80% of the plant below ground, penetrating to depths of 15 m or more where there may be moisture protected from capillary rise and evaporation.

In the Namib Desert, beetles and silverfish feeding on tussock grass (*Aristida*) are in turn fed upon by skinks, geckos and other lizards. Large ungulates like the dorcas gazelle and oryx form troops of up to twenty head in the southern Sahara. The number of species and individuals is much higher towards the wetter margins of the arid zone, especially in the vicinity of pools and lakes and inland deltas like the Okavango on the northern edge of the Kalahari.

The Bushmen

Few hunting peoples survive in the arid regions. The Bushmen of the western Kalahari are almost unique in this respect. They live much as their ancestors did millennia ago, except that they use iron instead of bone for their arrowheads and spears, and have a great liking for chewing tobacco. For food they depend on nuts, beans and roots, wild produce which has a high protein content and is nutritionally adequate. Fifty per cent of the diet of the !Kung Bushmen of Botswana comes from mongongo nuts (*Ricinodendron rautanenii*); the plant is drought resistant and the nuts can lie on the ground for twelve months without rotting. Occasionally the Bushmen kill a wildebeest or warthog and have a feast. A band of a dozen or so individuals can subsist adequately so long as two-thirds of its members are engaged in finding food for about a third of the time. The two basic necessities of food and water may not be found in the same place so that in the dry season, when the camp has to remain close to the waterholes, the food-gatherers may have to walk several kilometres to obtain adequate supplies. In that season an area of about 100 sq. km might supply the needs of about fifteen Bushmen. In the rainy season they move camp more frequently and are usually nearer their sources of food (Figs. 61, 62).

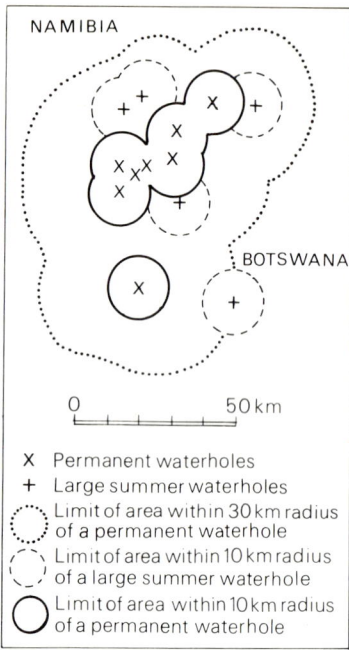

61 Intensity of land use and distance from permanent waterholes among the !Kung Bushmen of the Dobe area of north-west Botswana
The area within a 10 km radius of a permanent waterhole supports all this group of Bushmen for half the year; the area within a 10 km radius of a large summer waterhole supports most of these Bushmen for the rest of the year. None of these Bushmen camp or forage further than 30 km from permanent waterholes

Month	Jan	Feb	Mar	Apr	May	June	July	Aug	Sept	Oct	Nov	Dec
Season	Summer rains			Autumn dry			Winter dry			Spring dry	First rains	
Availability of water	Temporary summer pools everywhere			Large summer pools			Permanent waterholes only				Summer pools developing	
Group moves	Widely dispersed at summer pools			At large summer pools			All population restricted to permanent waterholes				Moving out to summer pools	
Men's subsistence activities	Hunting with bows, arrows and dogs throughout the year → Some gathering throughout the year →											
	Running down immature animals						Trapping small game in snares				Running down new-born animals	
Women's subsistence activities	Gathering mongongo nuts throughout the year →											
		Gathering fruits, berries and melons					Gathering roots, bulbs and resins				Gathering roots and leafy greens	
Relative subsistence hardship		Water–food distance minimal				Increasing distance from water to food					Water–food distance minimal	

Pastoralism

Just as game moves with the seasons, according to the availability of water and grass, so the early herdsmen followed a mobile existence, concentrating near rivers and lakes in the dry season. They inscribed or painted pictures of their cattle in rock shelters (where they can still be seen), and they then spread out more widely in the rains. Over a long period they drifted across the continent. The pastoralists of the semi-arid grasslands depended for their food on the milk and in some cases the blood from their cattle, and also on millet (*Pennisetum* spp.) which they grew for themselves or obtained from the sedentary cultivators. Some dug wells (or kept slaves for that purpose) and watered their herds in the dry season by drawing up water from depths of 100 m or more. They sold some stock locally but cattle were considered as wealth to be treasured rather than currency to be spent.

In the course of this century, pastoralists have become accustomed to selling their cattle to dealers who purchase mature beasts and assemble herds for trekking to market. The trade from the Niger bend into Ghana seems to have been stimulated by drought in the grazing lands around 1912–14 and later by the availability of rail transport. The demand for meat comes from the townspeople and the cocoa-growers of the coastal regions. From the Kalahari, cattle are trekked hundreds of kilometres from the Ghanzi area in north-west Botswana to a slaughterhouse and cannery at Lobatsi on the railway to Cape Town. In Botswana, Ghana and other countries, lorries are used increasingly, bringing the stock to market in better condition. Still, the prices paid to the pastoralists are low and middlemen collect much of the profit from the trade.

Numbers of livestock have increased very rapidly in this century. The number of pastoralists too has grown, and they have needed more animals to provide milk and bridewealth. Central governments have forbidden raiding and have dug wells which in some cases tap artesian water. Losses from disease have been reduced. Veterinary departments have inoculated cattle against rinderpest, especially during the 1960s when international campaigns attempted to eradicate the disease. With the clearing of the land for agriculture and the killing of a large number of game animals, areas formerly closed to pastoralists because of infestation with tsetse flies have become available to them at least for dry-season grazing. (Streamside thickets provide numerous breeding areas for the fly and the game animals are a reservoir of trypanosomes, the microbes which bring sleeping sickness to humans and the deadly *nagana* or trypanosomiasis to cattle and other livestock.) During the 1950s and early 1960s the Sahelian zone received more rain than usual. Cattle spread deeper into the arid zone and the risks of over-grazing and the spread of desert conditions were forcibly emphasised when severe droughts affected the Sudan and Sahelian zones in the period 1968–73. Cattle died in their hundreds, pastoralists lost their means of livelihood and desert conditions spread south.

Pastoralists in the Sahara and Somalia have depended mainly on camels and goats, which can better survive the severe arid conditions. The camels were important in long-distance trading; thousands of them were involved in the caravan trade between the Mediterranean lands, the date-palm (*Phoenix dactylifera*) oases of northern Algeria, Saharan salt quarries and towns south of the desert acting as entrepots for slaves and ivory from the savanna and forest lands. Activity has declined with the construction of railways and roads, and the oases that were used as bases by Touareg and Tibu nomads and raiders, with gardens under the date-palms worked by their serfs, are being abandoned. Now there is no sale for camels and raiding is less productive than formerly. Lorries call at the oases, roads link them to the outside world and their inhabitants have found work with oil-drilling teams. The demand for labour with the oil companies has slackened recently, though, and the people now seek employment in the towns at the desert margins. The breakdown of rural life is more dramatically portrayed in the arid regions than elsewhere in Africa, but is still far from dead. This poses the question of how much support should be given to the traditional systems and whether radical measures should be taken to re-orient economies and societies along modern lines.

Somali transhumance

In Somalia only 12% of the total land area of 660 000 sq. km is considered suitable for cultivation. Livestock production supports about 70% of the population and is the basis of the country's economy. Most of the livestock are reared by nomadic herders whose movements follow two general circuits from home bases near the coast. The northern coastal people move southwards into the Haud (Fig. 63a) while the eastern coastal people move westwards into the Doi. The specific routes depend on competition from rival herdsmen, the presence of natural barriers and human diseases, and variations in temperature. After spending the major dry season (Table 9) close to settlements with permanent water supplies – known as home wells – the northern Somalis set out to find fresh pastures and water supplies in the Haud, a plateau area on the borders of Ethiopia and Somalia. Constant crossing of the frontier

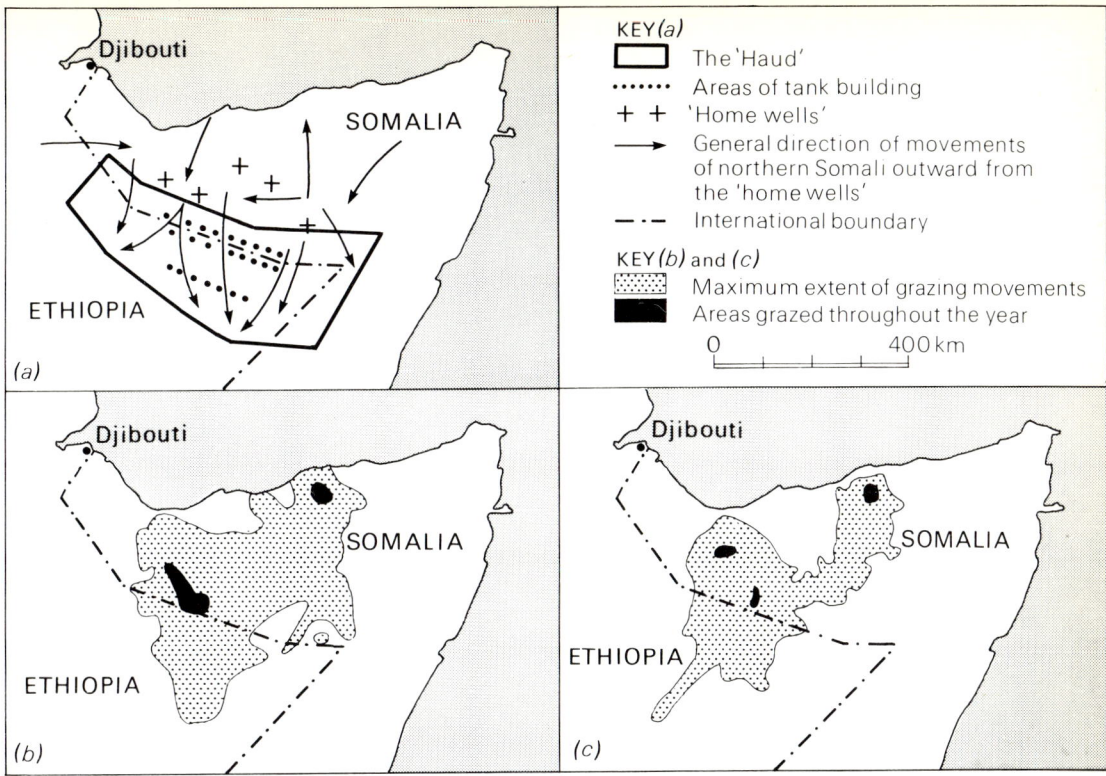

Table 9. Seasons in northern Somalia

Major rainy season	April to June
Minor dry season	July to August
Minor rainy season	September to November
Major dry season	December to March

63a Movement of northern Somali pastoralists in the Horn of Africa
63b, c The varying grazing areas of the Habr Yuni, a Somali group, in two successive years

between the two countries gives rise to international political disputes (Fig. 63b, c). Somali groups do not have particular rights to specific water or pastures; all are entitled to what is available. Life is very hard for these pastoralists; as one of their proverbs says, 'abundance and scarcity are never far apart; the rich and poor frequent the same houses.'

The number of sheep, goats, camels and people in one nomadic unit changes constantly, depending on present and potential future food and water supplies. Different distributions of stock occur within an area. Camels can browse on thorny bushes and exist for twenty days without water so young herdsmen can range up to 80 km from their camp when pasture and water are especially scarce. Other animals graze close to the camp, under the eyes of the older men. As pasture and water supplies deteriorate the herdsmen make their way back to the permanent water sources in the north, thus completing their annual circuit.

Attempts have been made to provide a more reliable water supply in the Haud. Covered, clay-lined tanks have been excavated in depressions to collect water which is sold to the pastoralists (see Fig. 63a). On a smaller scale, hollows in the ground have been lined with clay to help retain rainfall, but the high evaporation rates cause rapid losses and limit their usefulness.

64 The nomadic areas of the Arabs in the Sudan

Pastoralism in the Sudan Republic

A large proportion of the population of the Republic of the Sudan are also pastoralists (Fig. 64), and conditions in the north of the country are at least as severe as in Somalia. In the Sudan the Arab nomads who live to the west of the River Atbara follow the rains northwards in the middle of the year and return southwards to their home bases beside the rivers for the dry season. The government tries to control the movements of the herdsmen in order to allow the sedentary cultivators time to reap their crops before the herds arrive and thus prevent conflicts between them. The composition of the nomadic herds depends on the weather: in the dry areas of the north, camels are herded with sheep and goats, but in the wetter south, where pastures are more reliable, cattle are more important than camels. A different physical environment exists east of the River Atbara where hills and plains border the Red Sea. The humidity is greater, there are variations in temperature with altitude, and some areas have larger amounts of rainfall. The nomadic movements in this area reflect these features.

South of latitude 12°N the nomadic movements of the Nilotic peoples are a response to the seasonal changes in the water level of the White Nile, which affects the amount of dry land available. During the wet season, from April to December at this latitude, the people live in permanent settlements and cultivate crops on high ground above the flooded valley floors. The cattle are kept for much of the time in huts filled with smoke to keep away biting flies. Some grazing takes place around the villages, and as the floods recede the

65 Seasonal movements of the pastoral peoples of the southern Sudan

cattle are taken to new pastures at increasingly greater distances from the exhausted village pastures. In February the people move to camps beside the large rivers and permanent swamps, returning to their villages in April. The Sudanese authorities consider these people to be sedentary because the duration of their migration is less than in the areas further north although the distances they cover are as great (Fig. 65).

Irrigation

The Sudan Republic

The greatest changes in desert ecosystems have taken place where water has been brought from a distance, radically changing the productive potential. In Africa the largest river flowing into the desert is the Nile, which has been used for irrigating the delta and floodplain in Egypt for 5000 years. Egypt, however, is outside the tropics and we are concerned here with developments further upstream in the Sudan Republic.

The irrigation of the Gezira Plain south of Khartoum has proved to be one of the most successful agricultural development projects in tropical Africa. Because of the size of the projects and the costs involved the government has played a decisive role in this development of commercial agriculture. At the beginning of the twentieth century, after careful surveys, the British colonial administration of the Sudan decided to invest in a complex irrigation scheme on the Gezira Plain between the rivers Blue and White Nile. It planned to grow cotton to provide raw materials for British industry and a cash

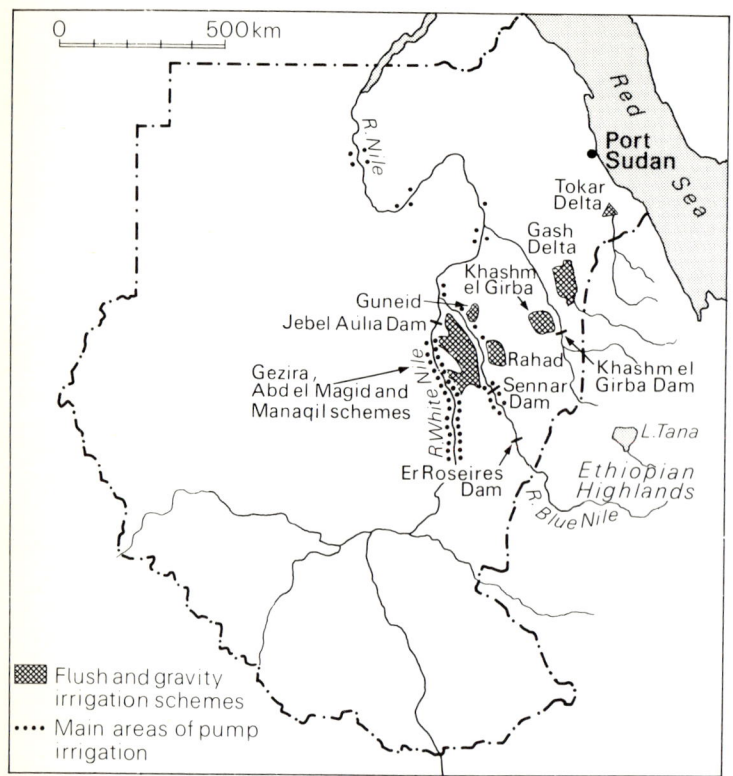

66 Irrigation schemes in the Republic of the Sudan

crop for the Sudanese. The initial scheme, which included the construction of the Sennar Dam, was completed in 1925. Subsequently the irrigated area has been extended and further dams built (Fig. 66). The gently sloping Gezira Plain, with its impermeable black clay soils, is extremely suitable for irrigation and allows the use of a standard layout of fields and canals. Water flows under gravity to the fields. The impermeability of the soils means little water is lost by seepage from the canals and the underground drainage of surplus irrigation water is unnecessary, although superficial drains are needed to take off surface water after heavy rain. The water of the Blue Nile is not heavily charged with salts and the accumulation of harmful salts such as sodium in the soil is not a problem here, as it is in many other irrigation schemes.

The farmers are annual tenants of the Sudan Gezira Board but the children of satisfactory tenants can inherit the tenancies. The tenant farmers are mainly 'westerners' from the western part of the Sudan Republic and Hausas from west Africa, some of whom were pilgrims on their way to or from Mecca who decided to earn money as labourers and eventually settled down to plant cotton for themselves. Each farmer is provided with four plots, totalling 16 hectares, in contiguous blocks of nine plots called 'numbers'. He is expected to live in a village close to his plots (Fig. 67). Each 'number' is cultivated as a unit, as directed by the Board managers. Before 1959, an agreement with Egypt on the use of the Nile waters severely restricted the amount the Sudan could use for irrigation; however, this is no longer the case. Maximum returns per unit of water were

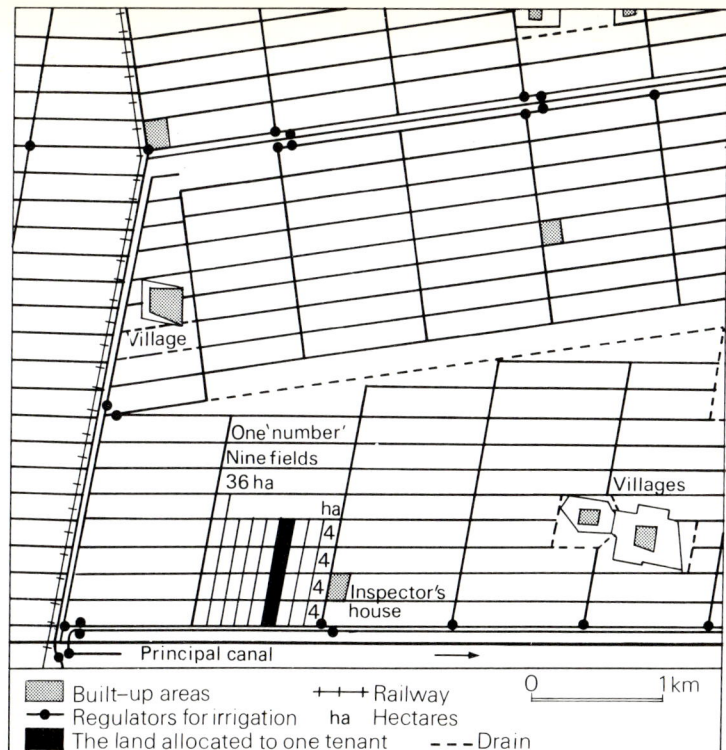

67 A typical layout of villages, canals and fields in the Gezira, Sudan

at that time more important than returns per unit of land so a cotton crop was, and still is, grown on a 'number' only twice in eight years (Table 10). The tenant has no choice in the plots he uses for commercial crops but he can grow what food he likes on fallow land. The Board provides such things as cotton seed, fertiliser, irrigation water, instructions and marketing facilities, while the tenant attends to the daily requirements of his individual plots, crops and irrigation channels. At harvest time, much additional labour from other areas is employed. Under the tenancy agreements 52% of the cotton crop goes to the Sudan Government and the Board in payment for the services provided and instead of taxes; the remainder including all the food crops belongs to the tenants. The cotton yields per hectare are fairly high (Table 11) and the tenants are prosperous. As they are unable to grow all their own food supplies they provide a market for produce from the surrounding unirrigated areas.

Table 10. Rotations in the Sudan

Year	Gezira	Other schemes
1	Cotton	Cotton
2	Fallow	*Sorghum*
3	Fallow	Fallow
4	Cotton	Cotton
5	Fallow	*Sorghum*
6	*Sorghum*	Fallow
7	Lubia[1]	Cotton
8	Fallow	*Sorghum*

[1] Lubia = *Dolichos lablab*, a legume

Table 11. The yields of cotton in some producing countries (in kilograms per hectare)

Country	Year 1966–7	1967–8	1968–9	1969–70	1970–1
Sudan	395	400	466	389	454
Uganda	88	71	92	101	85
USA	536	499	576	484	488
USSR	830	837	833	781	850
India	127	140	135	135	124

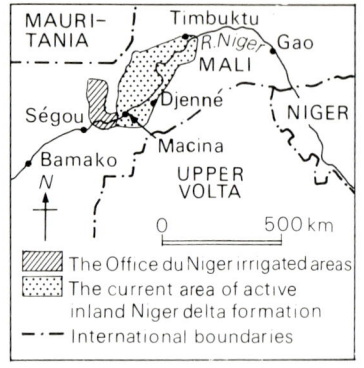

68a The Inland Niger Delta area in Mali
68b Irrigated areas of the Office du Niger, Mali

On new gravity irrigation schemes such as Khashm el Girba more water is available and hence the land is cropped more intensively so the farm size is smaller, from 6 to 8 hectares. The government still directs production. Other government investment has established controls for the natural flow of water in the Gash and Tokar deltas and pump schemes along the Nile and other rivers where the traditional shaduf and water wheel still raise water to many fields and market gardens. Wealthy private citizens also invest in pumped irrigation schemes, which are very profitable since the capital outlay can be recovered in three years. Tenants on private schemes receive half the profits from the crops grown.

Cotton is the main cash crop of the Sudan and it accounts for more than half its export earnings (Table 12). Although it is the world's second largest producer of long staple cotton, on new schemes like Rahad (see Fig. 66) short staple cotton is grown, and the government is encouraging crop diversification into cane sugar, groundnuts and vegetables. Export is mainly by rail to Port Sudan, but the development of an adequate all-weather road network is now essential.

Table 12. Cotton exports from the Sudan: their weight and relative value

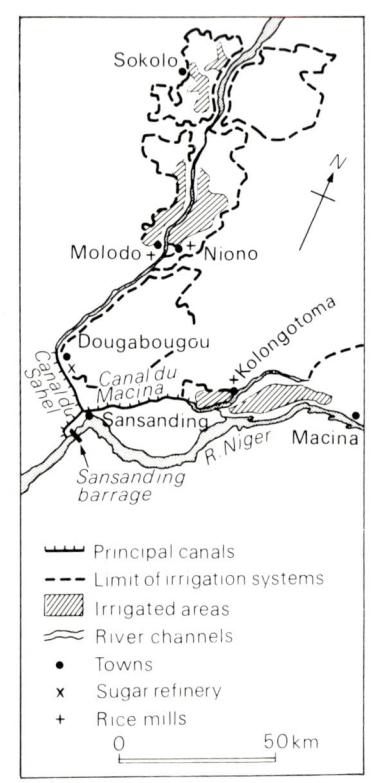

	1968	1969	1970	1971	1972	1973
Weight of cotton exports, in thousands of tonnes	183	172	231	240	247	225
Value of cotton as % of value of total domestic exports	59.8	57.8	63.6	56.3	59.3	55.4

Mali

In contrast with the Sudan, the French aim to create 'an island of prosperity' in the middle Niger basin of Mali has been much less effective. After a successful pilot project at Banguinéda near Bamako, a French public enterprise, the Office du Niger was created in 1932. This was to provide the capital investment and management of 900 000 hectares of irrigated land in the Inland Niger Delta, where 500 000 people could settle and cultivate rice (*Oryza sativa*) for food and cotton for cash (Fig. 68a). The local inhabitants are few in number and are mainly pastoral nomads or migrant fishermen; hence settlers had to be brought in from other parts of Mali or other countries such as heavily populated Upper Volta. The Sansanding

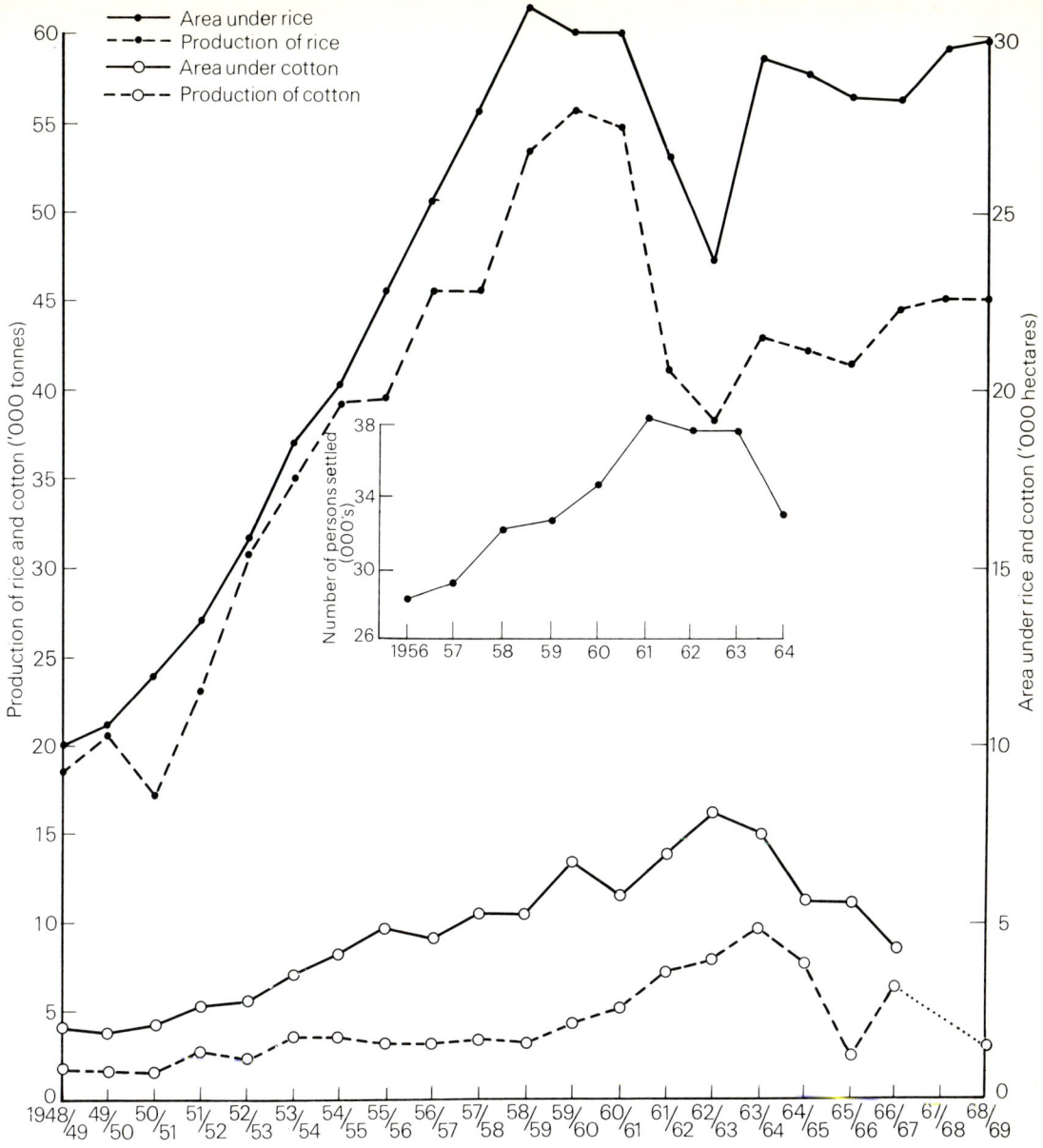

69 Office du Niger Scheme, Mali Cotton and rice area and production, 1948–69, and number of persons settled on the scheme, 1956–64

barrage was constructed to regulate the flow of water during the limited flood period and dykes, canals and former river channels were cleared to distribute the water (Fig. 68b). Much money has been invested in the scheme but the irrigated area is still only about 65 000 hectares. There have been changes of emphasis between farming with directed labour and family cultivation, the amount of land planted with cotton or rice, and the amount of mechanisation employed. Deficient technical information about local topography and climate has created difficulties with irrigation and drainage while the lack of settlers has prevented the extension of the cultivable area and prompted the management to organise the farming itself in some areas. Rice is grown continuously in most of the irrigated areas. Cotton is important only in the Niono area, where two years' cropping is followed by one year fallow. Some sugar-cane is also grown. Despite efforts to intensify production, yields are not high and opportunities for agriculture elsewhere in Mali have proved more attractive to most of the people (Fig. 69).

North-east Nigeria

At present plans are being put into effect to irrigate clay plains in north-east Nigeria bordering Lake Chad, using water pumped from the lake. The chemical composition of this water is not very different from that of the Blue Nile, the soils are comparable with those of the Gezira and there is considerable population pressure in parts of Nigeria which should provide an adequate supply of labour. Problems that are presented by the varying extent of the lake, which may flood installations one year and then recede out of reach the next, have yet to be finally solved but it seems likely that the scheme will go ahead. If it does, the local pastoral and sedentary people, the Shuwa Arabs and Kanuri, and the nomadic Fulani who visit the area seasonally, will find their way of life greatly altered. But with careful control the economic productivity of the region will be greatly increased, by using water as an input that would otherwise have been wastefully evaporated from the lake. In the long run, most of the local people will gain but, as usual, some will lose.

6

Mountain, river, lake and coastal lands

Mountains

As you go up a mountain the mean temperature diminishes by about 1 °C for every 150 m of ascent. At an altitude of about 2500–3000 m mean annual temperatures in tropical Africa are comparable to those of western Europe but the climate is very different overall. Temperature differences between day and night are much greater than between one season and another; the sun is higher in the sky for a longer period of the year and day length varies much less than in higher latitudes. As a result, the conditions for plant growth are of a special kind, differing from those at lower altitudes near by and from those of lowland areas in higher latitudes.

The equatorial high mountains, like the up-faulted mass of Ruwenzori alongside the western rift and the great volcanoes Elgon, Kenya and Kilimanjaro, display a zoning of vegetation which, as Fig. 70 shows, is related to altitude. The zones are fairly clearly marked but not entirely regular and vary considerably from one mountain to another. Savanna woodland on the plains merges into montane forest at a height of about 1500 m on slopes receiving more than about 1000 mm of rain. *Podocarpus* and juniper (*Juniperus* spp.) are among the characteristic species. With increasing altitude and rainfall, bamboo and other species become important, but the precipitation usually diminishes above 3000 m. The upper part of the forest at about 3500 m may be dominated by juniper, *Hagenia* and *Hypericum*. Above this the vegetation is usually dominated by giant heathers (*Erica* spp.) and giant-sized forms of *Lobelia*, *Alchemilla* and *Helichrysum*. Each of these zones of vegetation has its own assemblage of animals, from termites to birds and monkeys. Unfortunately they are all liable to be destroyed by human interference in the form of felling, burning, pasturing and cultivation. Some have been constituted nature reserves but many areas and assemblages remain at risk.

The high country between about 1500 and 2500 m is particularly well favoured. On the rainier slopes the trees grow tall but there is a smaller number of tree and animal species than in the lowland forest. The assemblages found on widely separated islands of forest have much in common. It has been suggested that such forests may have been continuous across the main high watersheds at some time in the past when temperatures during the glacial periods were several degrees lower than at present. A lowering of temperature of about 6 °C is likely to have occurred and this would have been sufficient to allow the linkage to be established. At the peak of the last glaciation it seems that rainfall totals were less than they are now in tropical Africa and possibly inadequate to support montane high forest, but the linkage could have taken place rather earlier when it was cooler than now but not much drier.

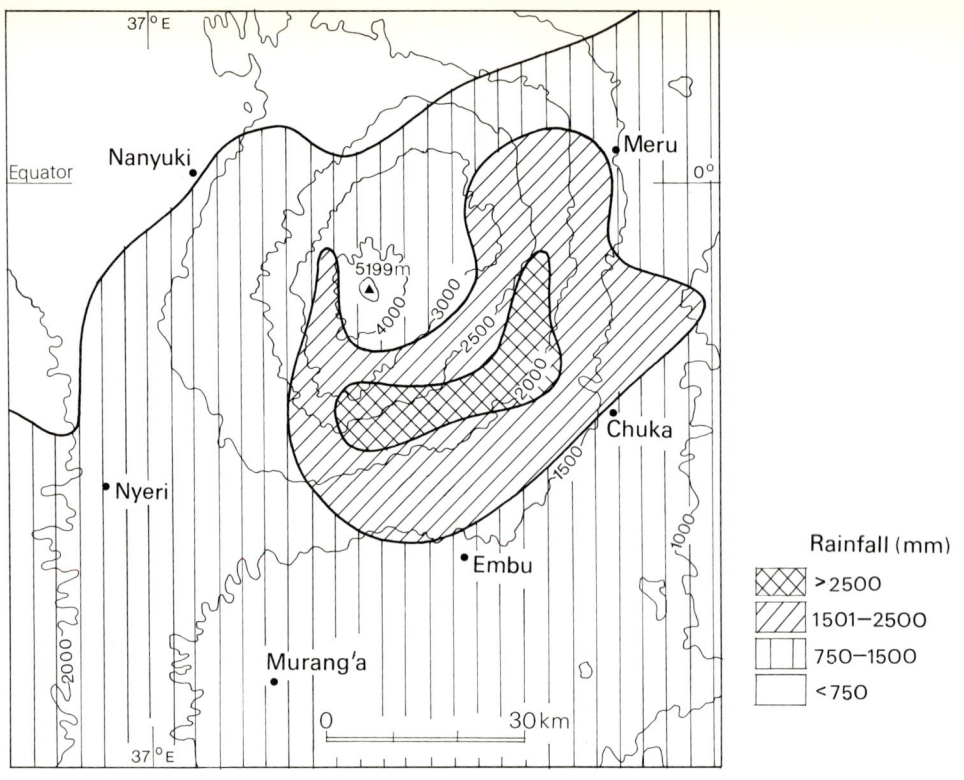

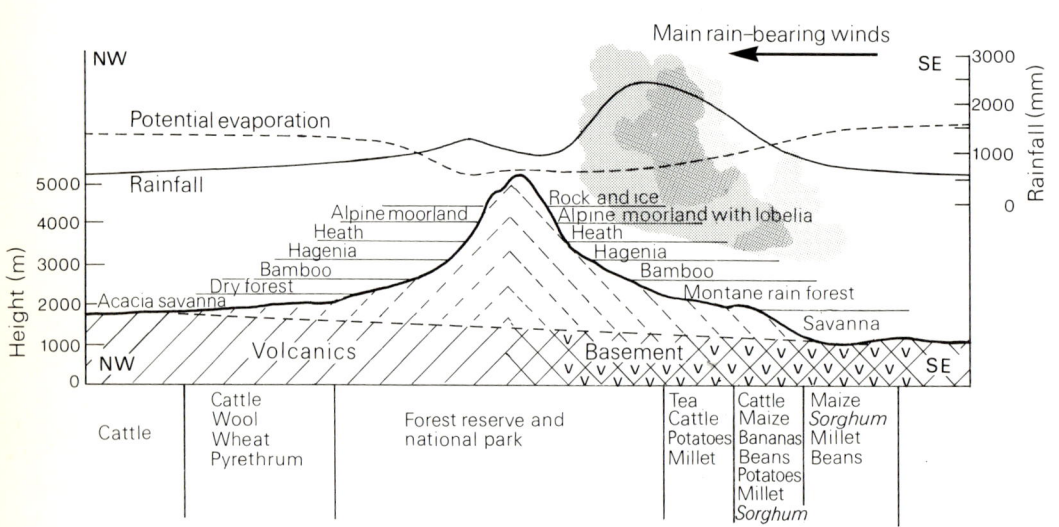

70 Altitudinal arrangement of rainfall and vegetation on Mount Kenya

In Kenya and Tanzania much of the montane high forest has been cleared or transformed by farming; hardly any remains in Ethiopia. Such country is particularly attractive to settlement by both Africans and Europeans. Not only is the climate pleasant, being sunny in the daytime and refreshingly cool at night, and the scenery outstandingly beautiful, but the land is very productive agriculturally, especially where the soils are derived from volcanic rocks. The contrasts in relief and soil characteristics over short distances, coupled with the variations in aspect and local climate, provide a large number of different ecological conditions which are ideal for mixed farming. A great variety of crops can be grown successfully, such as tea, coffee, fruit and vegetables and grains more typical of high latitudes. In fact the very desirable *arabica* coffee can be grown only above 600 m. Domestic animals thrive, tsetse flies being absent at this altitude, though there are diseases which can be harmful. The potential productivity of the montane forest ecosystem is high because gross photosynthesis reaches high levels and, what is more, respiration losses are kept down by the low night temperatures. Thus net productivity and the rate of storage in the form of timber are high, given sufficient water. Plantations of *Eucalyptus* in Ethiopia are notably high yielding.

Ethiopia
Large, highly dissected mountainous areas such as Ethiopia suffer from serious problems of accessibility. Roads are few, very costly to build and always at the mercy of the weather. It is not surprising, therefore, that the variety of both the scenery and the ways of life in the mountains of Ethiopia contrasts strikingly with most of the rest of tropical Africa. Three major farming systems are found within short distances of each other: nomadic pastoralism, permanent cultivation of ensete, (discussed later in this chapter), and rotational fallow cultivation of various grain crops. Ethiopian society is changing but until 1974 the political structure was very feudal and much of the land was owned by the Coptic Christian Church or wealthy landlords. Most farmers are tenants rather than holders of cultivation rights and changes in agriculture have taken place only very slowly.

The Amhara. The Amhara, who are the political dominant group of people in Ethiopia, live mainly in the central highlands at altitudes ranging from 1700 to 2800 m above sea level. They cultivate millet (*Eleusine* spp.) and barley (*Hordeum* spp.), which is much used for making beer, and particularly a cereal called t'ef (*Eragrostis abyssinica*), which is not grown as a food crop anywhere else in the world. T'ef is a very small grain but yields are quite large and it stores extremely well. It is used to make a form of bread called *injera* which is usually eaten with a peppery sauce called *wat*. T'ef has a high iron content and on milling for flour the wastage is only very small as compared with wastages in the milling of wheat.

Ox-drawn ploughs are used to break the soil before planting and four ploughings are usually required to prepare an adequate seed bed. The Amhara farmers weed their fields carefully to stop the young crops being choked and they harvest by hand, as ripe t'ef releases its grain very easily. Wheat and barley are grown at high altitudes and *Sorghum* and finger millet at lower levels, as well as beniseed and haricot beans (*Phaseolus vulgaris*), which are grown in association with t'ef. Animals, particularly cattle, are grazed on uncultivated areas during the day, thus supplying some manure to the fallow fields. They are stalled at night and, although fodder crops are not grown, t'ef straw is used as an animal feed. The stall manure is used mainly for fuel both for cooking and keeping warm in the cold evenings, but some is put on the fenced gardens which are close to the compounds and which are planted with spices, cabbages (*Brassica* spp.), *Cucurbita*, maize and gourds (*Lagenaria vulgaris*).

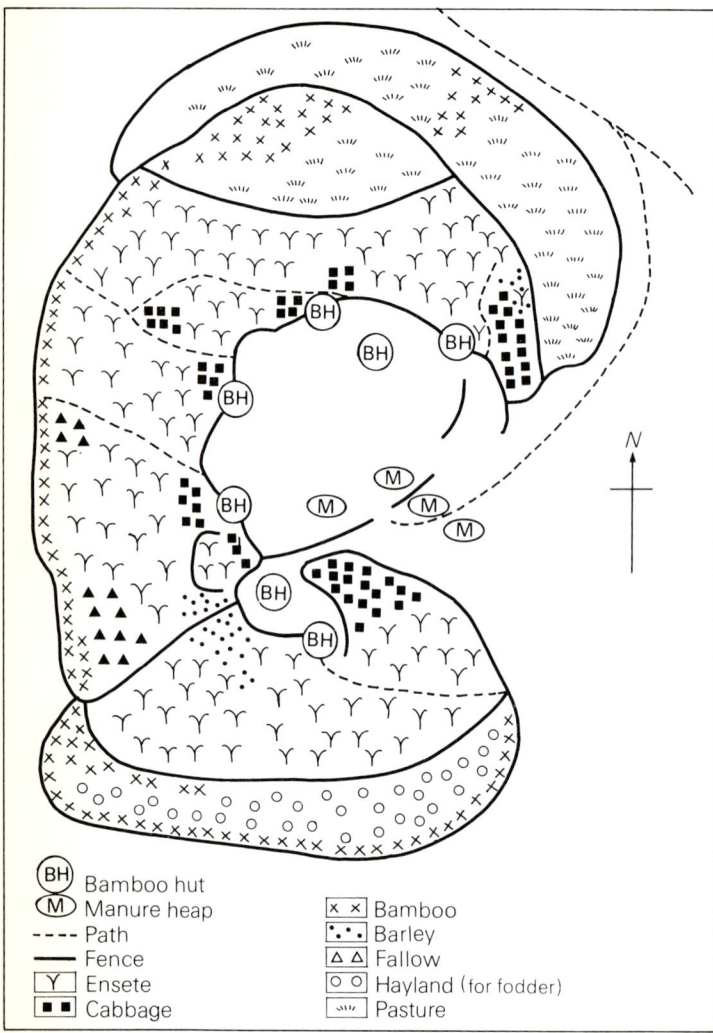

71 Typical land use in eastern Sidam Ethiopia

The Sidamo. In the moist highland zone of southern Ethiopia the major foodcrop is ensete, which resembles the banana plant but has inedible fruit. In this area the soils are volcanic, fertile and productive. Much of the land in the Sidamo country is permanently cultivated and the landscape is dominated by the fenced ensete plantations (Fig. 71). The trunk and the leaf sheaths, which are the important part of the ensete plant, are processed to form a highly nutritious, fermented starch flour which can be stored and a fibre which is sold for rope or thread. The plant is propagated from suckers taken from established plants and transplanted into carefully prepared nursery beds. After several years they are moved from these beds into the main plantation, where they remain until they are ready for harvesting. This usually occurs after nine years' growth. An average family may have 400 fully grown plants of which they may harvest 100 each year. Cattle and other animals are kept and stalled in huts at night but they are allowed out to fenced pastures during the day. Manure from the cattle huts and household ash are spread on the plantations and help to maintain high yields. Bamboo (*Arundinaria alpina*), citrus fruits, barley and cabbage are grown around the villages and as the area varies greatly in altitude there is much diversity in the other crops grown. Pasture grasses are good and some are cut for fodder. The contrast between the permanently cultivated land and the hill slopes is striking. The basaltic soils are productive but the runoff in some areas has eroded enormous gulley systems, particularly in areas where the underlying rocks are poorly resistant volcanic ash.

The Gisu

The Gisu who live on the slopes of Mount Elgon in Uganda also inhabit an area where the volcanic soils are very fertile and favourable for agriculture. Here the basic lavas have weathered to form soils which are rich in calcium, sodium and phosphates. These soils have a good texture and do not erode easily. The most important staple crop in this area is the banana, which is a perennial tree crop requiring humid conditions and rainfall well distributed throughout the year. The Gisu clear land and plant a crop of finger millet and beans, after which the soil is suitable for growing bananas. During the first year of the banana plant's growth, when it does not produce fruit, the Gisu plant other crops such as cotton, beans, finger millet and maize on the same plot. Later, only yams, cocoyams (*Colocasia esculentum*), vegetables and peppers are grown in the banana gardens. Manure is not used but refuse and leaf cuttings are left on the land. A well-managed garden produces crops which can be harvested throughout the year for many years. There are many varieties of banana; some are eaten fresh, some are made into beer, some are boiled and some are roasted, while there are any number of uses for the leaves, notably as umbrellas. Apart from the banana gardens, the Gisu cultivate other plots which may be cropped for about three years with various successions of finger millet, beans, maize, sweet potatoes and cassava, followed by two years fallow. Above 700 m *arabica* coffee, the chief cash crop, is planted and mulched with banana leaves. Higher still, above 1800 m, temperate vegetables, particularly potatoes (*Solanum tuberosum*), can be grown and here there are limited pastures for large herds of cattle, sheep and goats. Alpine pastures exist above 3500 m and these are grazed during dry weather. The number of people living in the area is large and pressure on the land is becoming a problem.

Around the bases of the mountains in east Africa are savannas where flat-topped *Acacias* are the characteristic plant. In the drier regions, around Marsabit in northern Kenya and down towards the Afar depression of Ethiopia, the montane forest and savanna degenerate to desert scrub below about 1000 m. It is possible to drive in a few minutes from cool green highlands with peasants harvesting barley to dusty plains where nomadic herdsmen lead their flocks and herds between the widely spaced wells. Changes are taking place by degrees in the drier piedmont country. The rivers of the highlands are being harnessed for hydro-electric power; water stored behind the dams and issuing from the tail-races of the turbines can be led to irrigate sugar-cane and cotton.

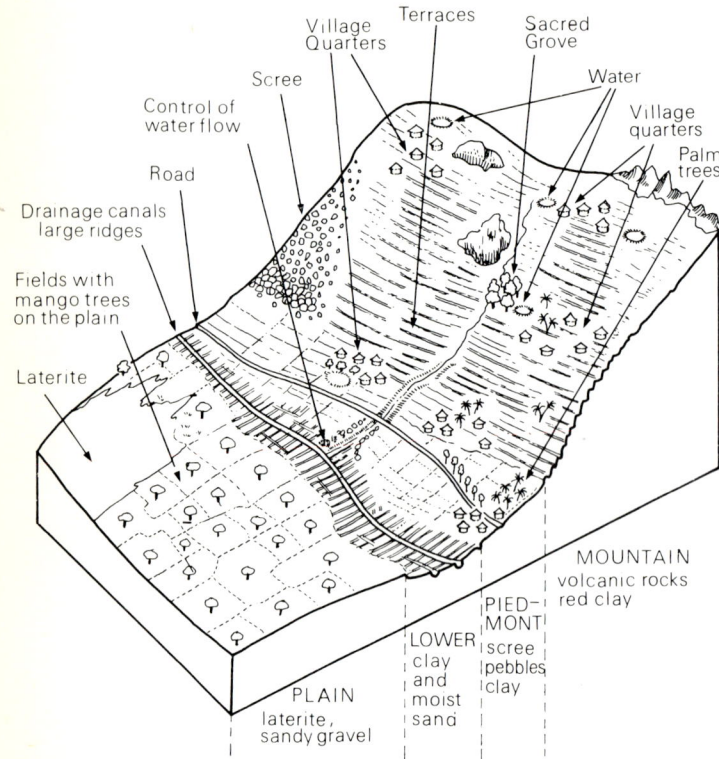

72 Block diagram of typical Kabrai country in Togo

The Kabrai

In west and central Africa, from Togo through Darfur in the Sudan Republic to Ethiopia, a string of hill settlements has been established by groups of people who had retreated to rocky massifs in order to defend themselves against invaders. In these areas the inhabitants are restricted by the rocky environment to limited pockets of cultivable soil but by careful techniques they manage to keep the soil under continuous cultivation. The Kabrai of northern Togo are one such group. Given the rocky nature of the area the population densities, which reach 80 persons per sq. km in some localities, are very high. Kabrai homesteads are dispersed over the intensively cultivated hillsides. Cultivation is concentrated in pockets of red clay soil which occur between irregular outcrops of hard grano-diorite rocks. The Kabrai protect these pockets of soil with terrace walls made of rocks and they build stone walls along the banks of streams to control the flow of water and prevent erosion (Fig. 72). The terraced land produces two crops of millet (*Pennisetum* spp.) each year and fertility is maintained by the application of manure, which is collected in pits (Fig. 73). Stall-fed sheep, goats, pigs and cattle contribute to the manure supply, which is mixed with household waste and spread on the gardens close to the homesteads. The main fields lie further from the dwellings and are cultivated during the wet season for *Sorghum*, the staple crop, and groundnuts, a cash crop. Conservation methods are employed on these fields also. Compost, leguminous foliage and some manure are dug into the soil, the crops are weeded very carefully and the people make every

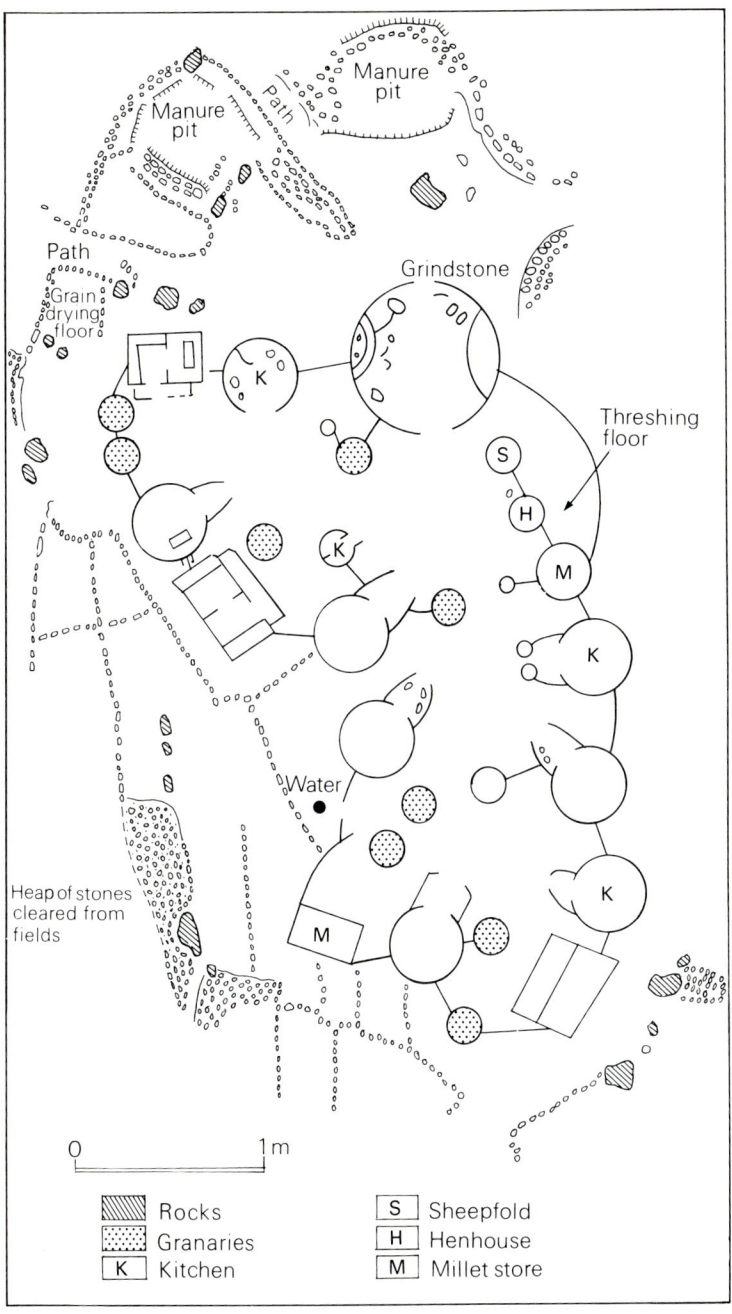

73 A Kabrai homestead

effort to destroy insect pests. The Kabrai also cultivate fields down on the plains which are cleared during the dry season and dug into mounds where yams are grown in the wet season (Fig. 74). Vegetables and groundnuts are sown on the sides of the mounds and rice between them. After the harvest the mounds are flattened and subsequent crop successions follow two main patterns: yams, cassava, fallow; or yams, sorghum and groundnuts for two years, then fallow. In water-logged areas the Kabrai dig drainage ditches and grow millet

Hypothetical cross-section of area			
Physical environment	Shelf or ledge	Mountain side	Plain
Field type	Compound garden	Main field	Out field
Cultivation system	Permanent cultivation	Permanent cultivation	Rotational cultivation
Maintenance of fertility	Animal manure Household refuse Compost	Green manure	Fallow
Cropping pattern	2 crops per annum	1 crop per annum	1 crop per annum for two years, then four years fallow
Crops	Early and late millet (*Pennisetum* spp.) Maize (*Zea mays*) Cocoyam (*Colocasia* spp.) Tobacco (*Nicotiana* spp.) White and black beans (*Kerstingiella geocarpa*) Spinach (*Ipomoea* spp.) Okra (*Hibiscus esculentus*) Pepper (*Capsicum* spp.) Yam (*Dioscorea* spp.) *Sorghum*	*Sorghum* Groundnuts (*Arachis hypogaea*) Millet Beans Yam	Yam Rice (*Oryza* spp.) Vegetables Okra Spinach Groundnuts Earthpeas (*Voandzeia subterranea*) Cassava (*Manihot utillissima*) Millet Beans *Sorghum*

74 Diagram of the Kabrai agricultural system

and groundnuts on ridges. With the coming of peaceful conditions in colonial times many hill people have abandoned this arduous terrace cultivation and have taken to rotational fallow cultivation on the near-by plains. The Kabrai settlements on the East Mono Plain are an example of this.

In the Sahara the desert mountains themselves are rocky and sparsely settled. On the higher parts of Tibesti and Hoggar, sweet-smelling shrubby plants grow, including Mediterranean species that seem to have survived from a cooler and more humid period. Settlement is concentrated at a small number of oases on the wadi floors where rock barriers bring water to the surface of the sediments — water that can be used for stock and to irrigate date palms and gardens yielding millet and vegetables.

Riverine areas

A distinct characteristic of tropical rivers is the presence of rapids or falls along their course, such as the Kabelega (Murchison) Falls (Fig. 75) on the River Nile in Uganda, the Victoria Falls on the River Zambezi bordering Zambia and Rhodesia or the Félou Rapids on the River Sénégal near Kayes in Mali. Some of these falls are used for hydro-electric power production, for instance the Lunsemfwa Falls

75 Kabelega (Murchison) Falls, Uganda

which supply electricity to the Zambian copper mines. Rapids and falls are a hindrance to the use of rivers as major lines of communication although much local use is made of rivers of sufficient size. In some areas like the creeks of the Niger Delta, boats are the only means of reaching some villages. River transport plays a significant part in main-line communications in Zaïre but each section is limited in extent and connected by road or rail, which involves frequent loading and unloading of freight.

Many of the rivers outside the humid forest lands are dry for half the year, stream beds being occupied by running water only after heavy storms and towards the end of the rainy season. The discharge of the large rivers increases as the rainy season progresses, the seasonal floodwaves move downstream and water levels rise in swamps and lakes along their course (Fig. 76). The great seasonal variation in river levels is a further obstacle to the use of water for transport and other purposes. In order to use the rivers for irrigation and power production dams and barrages are essential.

In savanna regions riverine lands can be cultivated during both the wet and the dry seasons. Swamp rice (*Oryza sativa*) is grown on flooded land during the wet season and valuable crops of upland rice, sugar and vegetables can be grown in the dry season. Pastoralists such as the Nilotic peoples mentioned in Chapter 5 make use of the riverine grazing, and people such as the Bozo of the Inland Niger Delta area specialise in fishing. The Bozo move from one fishing ground to another according to the season, setting up temporary settlements and constructing fence traps.

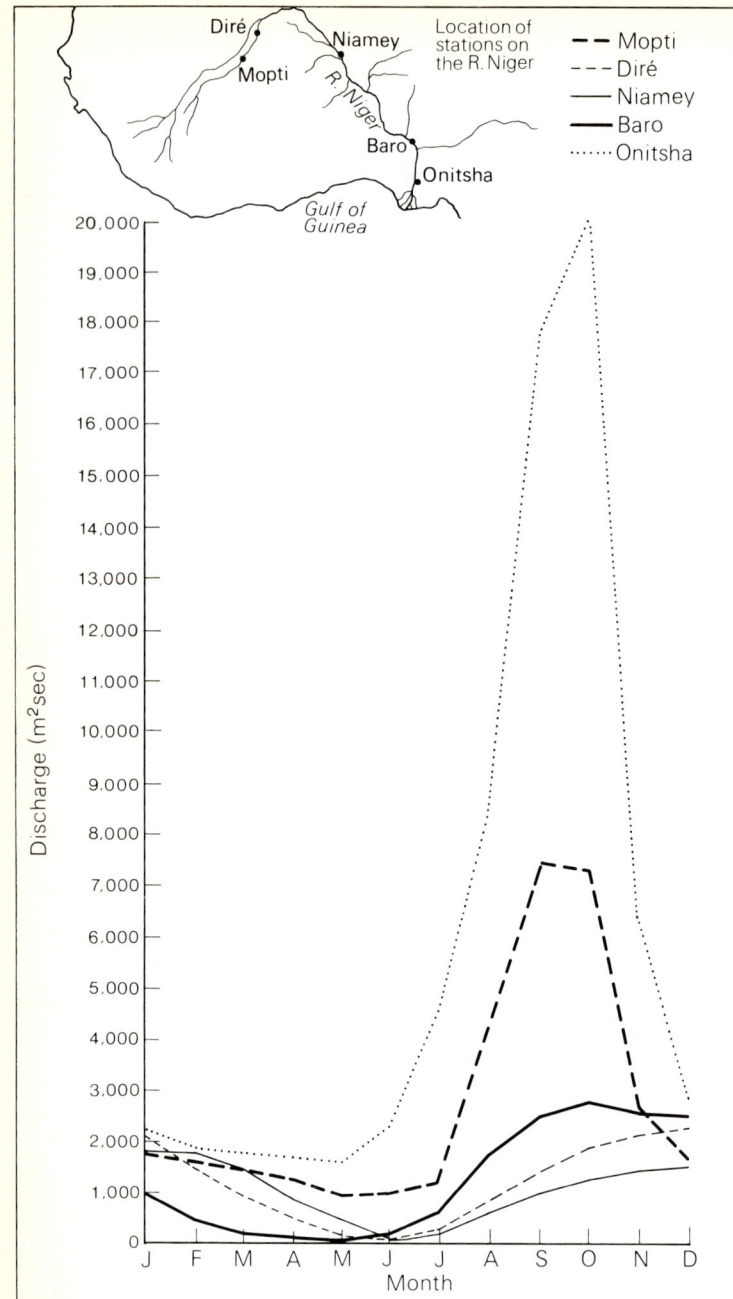

76 Mean monthly flow discharges for stations on the River Niger

Vegetation grows readily by water courses and, in savanna areas, gallery forests along the lines of streams provide breeding places for insects which transmit diseases. Mosquitoes, which carry malaria (Fig. 77), yellow fever and filaria, breed in water; the *Simulium* fly, which is the carrier for river blindness (onchocerciasis), breeds in turbulent streams; and snails such as *Bulinus* and *Biomphalaria* which transmit bilharzia (schistosomiasis) (Fig. 78) live in gently flowing water. Consequently human settlements are not concentrated along rivers in tropical Africa except in the arid zone or the flat forest country. The rivers are used for drinking water, cooking and washing but the frequency of contact between humans and the vectors of diseases is reduced a little by siting houses away from water.

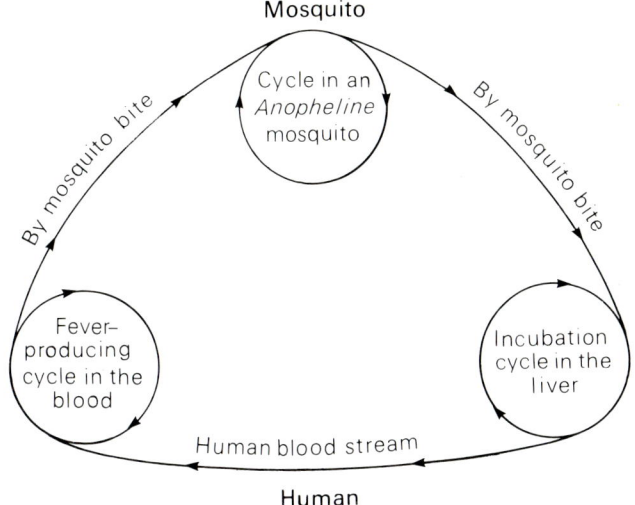

77 Life history of the malaria parasite

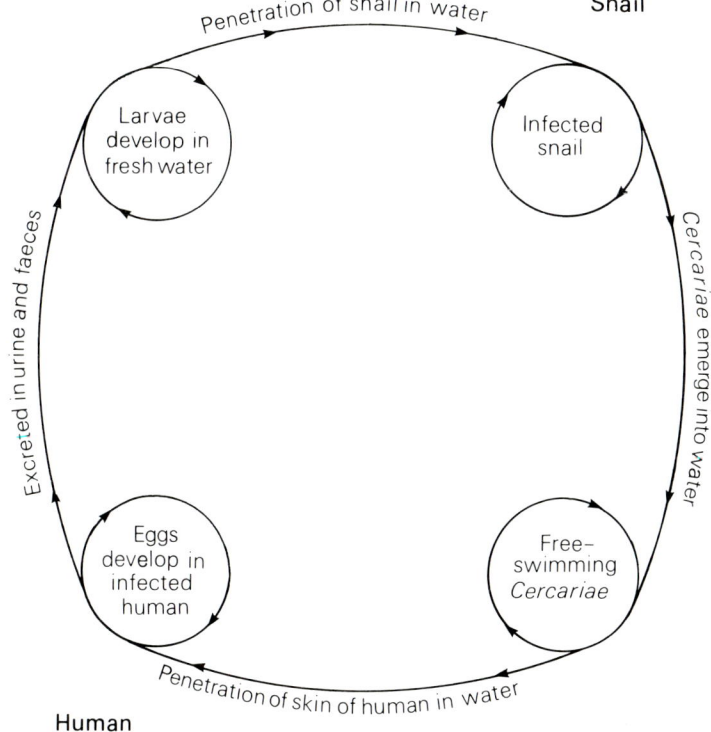

78 Life history of the schistosome in bilharzia

The lack of adequate sanitary arrangements and piped water supplies in most rural areas results in the transmission of numerous diseases which, although not fatal, sap the energy of the people.

Health facilities are improving slowly and campaigns to eradicate some diseases such as smallpox are well under way. In the case of malaria, it is possible to eradicate the disease more easily in areas such as east and central Africa where it occurs seasonally than in west Africa where it occurs continuously throughout the year. In areas of endemic malaria, although the adult population develops an immunity to the disease, the death rate among children aged between six months and five years is very high, between 5 and 15%. Over a million people are estimated to suffer from onchocerciasis in the Upper Volta River basin alone and many thousands of these sufferers are actually blind. The World Health Organisation has launched a special onchocerciasis control programme in the seven most badly affected countries: Benin, Ghana, Ivory Coast, Mali, Niger, Togo and Upper Volta. Aerial spraying of inaccessible rivers with insecticides to control the *Simulium* fly is a major feature of the programme. Schistosomiasis has increased in incidence with the building of irrigation works in many parts of Africa, since the lakes and slow-moving canals provide ideal breeding grounds for the snail vectors. Within three years of the creation of the lake behind the Kainji Dam in Nigeria, the proportion of the population around the lake affected by schistosomiasis had doubled.

Some groups of tsetse flies such as *Glossina palpalis* are found particularly in waterside vegetation. Human deaths from sleeping sickness are now rare although there was an outbreak of the disease in Ethiopia in the late 1960s, when many deaths were reported. In the past people were moved out of areas of particular danger to safer locations; the Anchau resettlement project in northern Nigeria in the 1940s was one such scheme. Nowadays the breeding grounds of tsetse flies are sprayed with pesticides, game animals (which are a reservoir of trypanosomes) are killed or controlled, cases of sleeping sickness are treated with drugs, and settlements are re-sited on cleared higher ground. Trypanosomiasis among cattle is still a very serious problem. The quality and number of cattle able to graze in tropical Africa are restricted by the disease and hence meat production is seriously limited. It is thought that if the disease could be controlled effectively the cattle population could be doubled, but this might lead to rapid deterioration of grazing lands.

Lakes and their shores

Most tropical African lakes are on the floors of rift valleys or in the central areas of large, structural sedimentary basins. The former are very deep in some cases: the bottom of Lake Tanganyika, for example, drops 1470 m only 4 km from the shore — which itself is 700 m above sea-level. The lakes in sedimentary basins are usually shallow but may be quite extensive; Lake Chad, as an example, has a mean depth of about 4 m and varies in area from about 10 000 to 25 000 sq. km according to the supply of water brought in by rivers entering from the south. In addition to such large bodies of water there are small lakes, especially in the vicinity of the rift valleys, in volcanic craters and calderas.

Most of the large lakes overflow to the sea, Tanganyika to the River Zaïre (formerly Congo), Victoria to the River White Nile, Malawi (formerly Nyasa) to the rivers Shiré and Zambezi. Turkana (formerly Rudolf), Chad and Rukwa do not overflow at present but they did so between 12 000 and 5000 years ago. At that time Lake Chad was enormously extended and overflowed via the River Benue to the River Niger; Lake Turkana, fed from lakes Stefanie (or Chew

Bahir), Chamo and Abaya, overflowed to the River White Nile. In the preceding arid period they were all much smaller. Chad dried up completely and its floor was covered with sand dunes; Lake Victoria provided no supply to the White Nile and the Sudd of the southern Sudan Republic was probably savanna with saline pools. The history of their oscillations and inter-connections helps to explain the assemblage of fish species found in them today.

The levels of the lakes which have no outflow vary markedly from year to year and season to season according to the rainfall. Evaporation from the catchments is always high and when this is subtracted from the rain, very little water remains to enter the lakes in dry years. Naivasha, Chilwa and Stefanie have been known to dry up completely; the floor of Stefanie was dry for most of the first half of this century. The environment provided by certain coastal lagoons, such as those near the mouth of the River Volta in southeast Ghana, is equally variable. When the lagoons dry out the people are able to harvest salt from their floors; then comes a period when brackish water floods them and fish can be caught in abundance.

Temperatures being high throughout the year and mean daily temperatures falling below 4 °C only at altitudes above 3000 m, lakes more than a few metres deep tend to become thermally stratified. This means that circulation is restricted, with warm water on the surface and the denser colder water stagnating at depth. Overturn of the water may take place only once a year, when the surface layers are chilled in the cool season, if there is one, or as a result of strong winds. Plankton and its consumers live in the surface layers. As they die and sink there is a strong tendency in the deeper lakes for nutrient salts to accumulate in the muds at the bottom and for the water below a depth of a few metres to be depleted of oxygen and unfavourable for fish life. Surface waters are also depleted of nutrients and depend on salts brought in by rivers and precipitated from the atmosphere in dust and rain. Productivity of the deeper lakes is not very high in many cases as compared with the shallow ones.

The most productive lake ecosystems from the fisherman's point of view are the shallow ones like Lake George in Uganda, Lake Chad where the Buduma people fish from papyrus boats, and the swamp lakes such as the Bangueulu swamps in Zambia. The fish breed at the end of the rains when water levels reach their maxima, flooding grassy plains where the young fish can readily find shelter from predators. Plankton growth can take place within a high proportion of the lake water, depending on its turbidity and the depth to which light can penetrate. Most important, the water circulates as a result of wind drag on the surface, bringing nutrients up to the top and preventing de-oxygenation. Under such conditions the fish attract large numbers of predatory birds as well as fishermen and the whole system is highly productive.

Large shallow lakes without outlets, like Lake Chad, do not necessarily become salt lakes, in spite of the fact that the rivers supplying them are constantly bringing in dissolved salts and material in suspension. It seems that the salts are taken up by plankton and plants or take part in complicated reactions with substances in the mud on the bottom and become trapped in the sediments that accumulate, while the lake water remains relatively fresh. This is one of the factors of importance in allowing the waters of Lake Chad to be used for irrigation.

The lakes in tropical Africa have not been drained to any great extent as yet. In the future the demand for more water for irrigation or industry and land for agriculture may lead to the canalisation of water through some of the great swamps. Obvious candidates for treatment are the Sudd, in the Republic of the Sudan, where half the discharge of the River White Nile is lost by evaporation, and the Okavango swamps, in Botswana, which reduce the rivers entering it to little more than a trickle at the outflow in some years.

The shores of the more productive lakes were favourable living sites for early man in Africa. His remains are widely found in the eastern arm of the rift valley system from the Olduvai Gorge in northern Tanzania, to the borderlands of Lake Turkana and the Afar depression in Ethiopia. Early fishermen with their simple nets and hooks probably made little impression on the lake ecosystems. More recent activities are having far-reaching consequences.

The hunting of predators, notably crocodiles, has much reduced their numbers. There are fewer creatures like hippopotamus, an animal that can be important in the cycling of nutrients because it grazes on land and defecates in lakes, where it spends much of the day-time, thereby transferring nutrients from land to water. Nylon nets, introduced in recent years, have enabled greater catches of fish to be taken in a shorter time. Outboard motors and large powered boats have allowed fishing far out into the big lakes. Total catches have increased and then, in some cases, have exceeded the maximum sustainable yield and declined.

Processing methods have also begun to change. Catches from Lake Chad and most other lakes are dried in the sun or smoked over wood fires, to preserve them for sale in distant markets. The efficiency of the methods has been improved by using new types of ovens, and refrigeration plants are used at Lake George.

Some lakes have been modified by engineering works. The Owen Falls Dam now controls the discharge from Lake Victoria. Other lakes have been created by damming rivers. The most extensive are Lake Volta, which floods 8500 sq. km, and Lake Nasser, 5000 sq. km. Both reach depths of over 70 m.

The filling of man-made lakes is accompanied by an explosive growth of animal and plant populations. This is as a result of the creation of new habitats and the introduction of organic material into the lake system at the advancing shoreline. The flooding and subsequent decay of trees and grasses release soil nutrients into the water. Large aquatic plants may occupy wide areas. One such was the *Salvinia auriculata*, a kind of water lily, which covered a large part of Lake Kariba. River species may not be able to tolerate the new conditions and are replaced by relatively rare species or by new ones deliberately introduced. Living conditions in the lake may be peculiar on account of the drowned woodland and violent fluctuations of level as water is stored in the rains and then drawn down by several metres in the dry season. The Volta Lake has provided a livelihood for a large number of Ewe fishermen who have migrated to the area and make good catches.

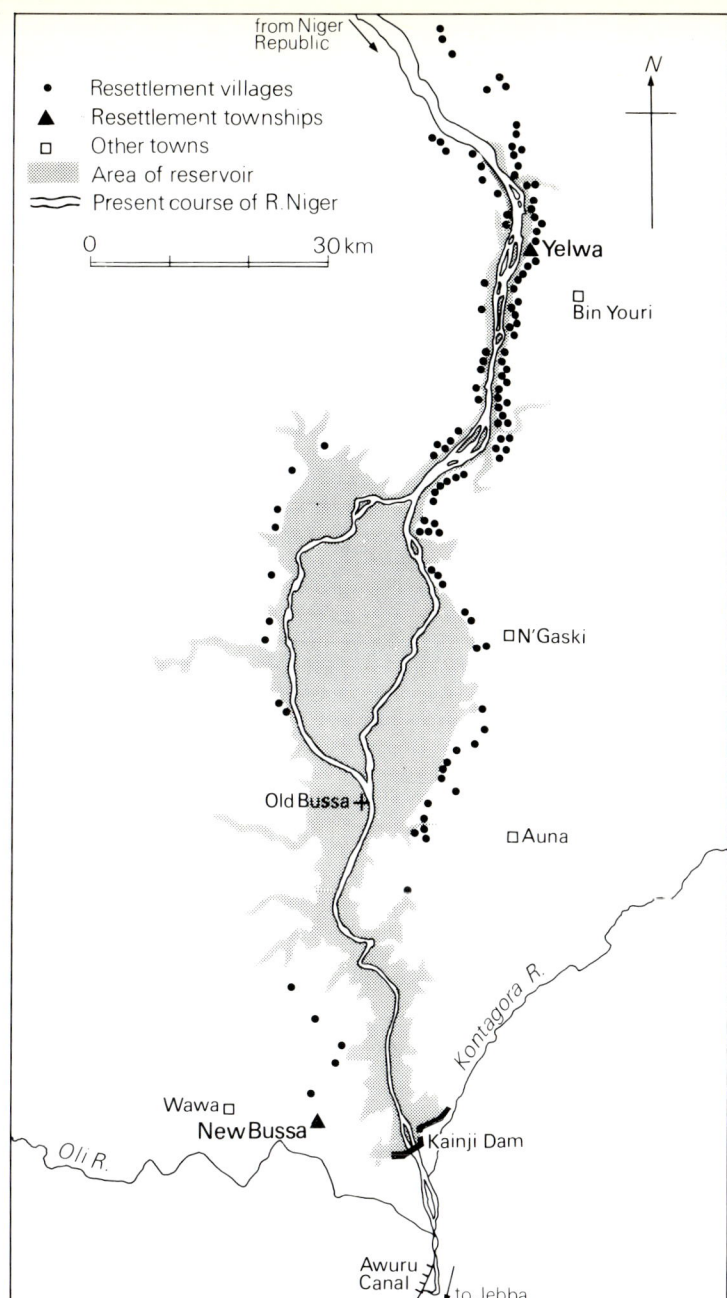

79 The Kainji reservoir and the re-settlement scheme, Nigeria

There are dangers of rural life being disrupted by river development schemes creating large lakes. About 85 000 persons were displaced by the creation of Lake Volta and 50 000 by the creation of the lake behind the Kainji Dam in Nigeria. Attempts were made to resettle the people (Fig. 79) but they found great difficulty in adapting themselves to quite new environments in unfamiliar surroundings. Damming the main stream produces stagnant water where malarial mosquitoes and snails carrying bilharzia are able to multiply, while building small dams in Upper Volta has transformed every weir into a breeding ground for the *Simulium* fly, which transmits onchocerciasis. Some people gain from the developments; others suffer. This is the inevitable result of change and it is important to ensure that the actual benefits exceed the real costs of development.

Coastal areas

The tropical African coastline, compared with that of Europe and south-east Asia, is regular, lacking deep estuaries and long promontories. Islands in the general region of the continent, with the exception of Madagascar, are small, though in some cases heavily settled. Low cliffed coasts occur locally, but the characteristic features are the mangrove swamps of the deltas, notably that of the River Niger, and the long sandy barrier beaches, built up by breaking waves with a long fetch, and separated from the mainland by long, narrow lagoons. Coral coasts are found only along the Indian Ocean. Estuaries are commonest in Gabon and between southern Senegal and Guinea.

Fishing

Some coastal peoples are very dependent on the sea and its resources, particularly in west Africa. North of Dakar the fish are those of the north Atlantic such as sea bream (*Dentex macropthalmus*) and mullet (*Mugil* spp.). Modern deep-sea fishing takes place from ports such as Nouadibou (Port Etienne) and European fishing vessels also operate in these waters. Very large catches are made by Russian trawlers, which can be accused of overfishing the area. Traditional African deep-sea fishing is rare because of the lack of navigational aids and large enough boats in the local technologies. Along the coast a Berber group fish, drying much of their catch for sale inland. South of Dakar lie the southern Atlantic fisheries where sardines (*Sardinella* spp.) and shad (*Ethmalosa* spp.) are the major constituents of the catch. Different coastal peoples, including the Serer, the Baga, the Fanti and the Ewe engage in fishing here.

The Ewe of Ghana and Togo operate all along the west coast from Sierra Leone to Angola. They form companies which contract to work for the owner of a net, usually a seine net, for a season. There are different specialist jobs within the company such as company secretary, canoe captain, net repairer and so on. The more responsible jobs earn a larger share of the profits of the enterprise. All members receive living expenses and accommodation while working for the company and a share of the profits at the end of the season. Women associated with the companies are responsible for preserving the fish by smoking them over wood fires or salting them. They then market the preserved fish, much of which is traded inland to the forest areas where animal protein is in short supply. Salt for preserving the fish is evaporated from sea water along the coastal lagoons. Small fish unsuitable for sale are used in the Volta Delta area as fertiliser, where they contribute to the production of high-value crops such as shallots. In the lagoons and estuaries of the tropical African coast, fences and baskets are constructed to trap the fish moving with the tides. Crustaceans such as shrimps and crayfish are also caught here. Some traditional fishermen have adopted nylon nets and mounted outboard motors on their canoes in recent years (Table 13). The canoe fishermen, however, are coming up against competition from highly capitalised fishing fleets operating from the main ports and especially the factory ships from Japan and the USSR. (The Russians increased their sale of frozen fish to the Ivory Coast from 10 000 tonnes in 1970 to 100 000 tonnes in 1976.)

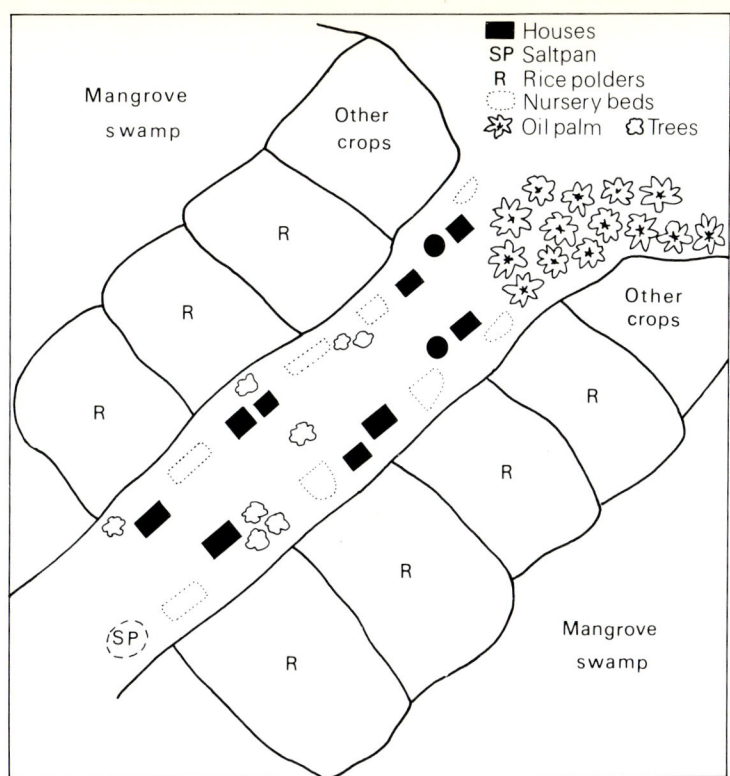

80 Plan of a Baga settlement and land use in Guinea

Table 13. Output of Ghanaian marine fisheries, 1966–71 (in thousands of tonnes)

	1966	1967	1968	1969	1970	1971
Canoe catch	25.2	39.9	33.3	60.2	90.0	113.3
Motorised fishing vessels' catch	49.3	63.4	60.8	80.8	67.6	68.3
Total catch	74.5	103.3	94.1	141.0	157.6	181.6

Coastal farming

The sandy soils of the coastal areas often support coconut (*Cocos nucifera*) plantations. Settlements among the trees depend on wells dug down to freshwater aquifers resting on top of denser salt water; these are liable to contamination if too much is extracted. Cultivation is difficult along the coast because of flooding but the Baga, who live among the drowned estuaries of the 'Rivières du Sud' in Guinea, are one of the few African groups who traditionally grow swamp rice on reclaimed marshland. The only other area in tropical Africa where swamp rice is a traditional rather than an introduced crop is in Madagascar, where its cultivation owes much to the strong Indonesian elements in the population.

Tidal ranges of more than 3 m seem to be necessary for coastal swamp rice cultivation to be successful, since this measurement limits the area cultivated in this way on the Guinea coast. Settlements are on sand bars or ridges of firm ground which are frequently linear in shape (Fig. 80). Between these ridges are marshy hollows where mangroves (*Rhizophora racemosa*) grow. These marshy areas are reclaimed over a period of three years to form fields. The mangrove trees and particularly the mangrove roots are cleared away

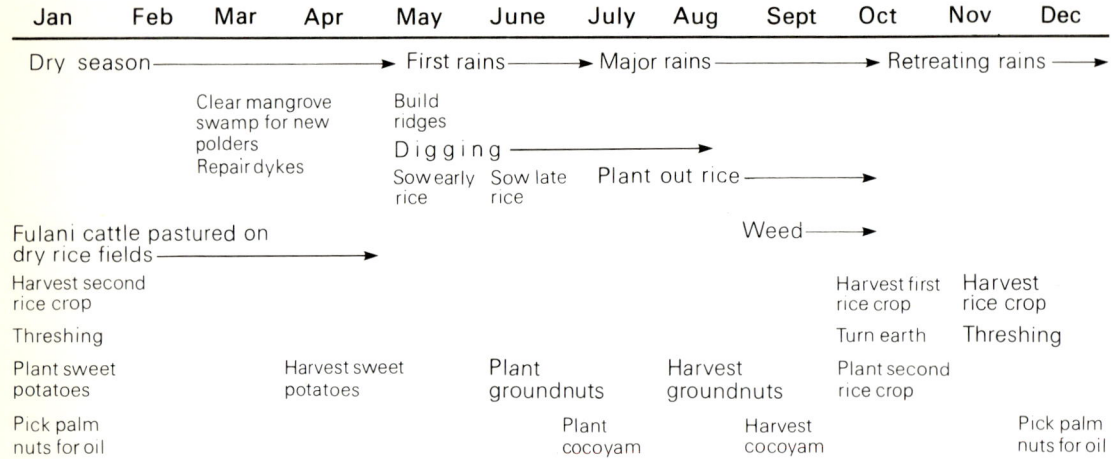

81 Calendar of agricultural activities among the Baga of Guinea

during the dry season when water levels are low. This is very hard work. A wall dyke is constructed round the proposed field to exclude salt water and it is closed with timber floodgates. The field is then left so that rainwater can wash out of the soil the excessive amounts of salt there, which would otherwise kill the crops. The dykes and gates have to be kept in good repair to prevent the sea flooding in when the tide rises and depositing further salt. When the plot is free of salt and ready for use, the Baga men turn the soil with a special long-handled iron-shod spade in order to dig in the weeds and expose the lower soil to the air. They then build the soil into ridges while the women sow prepared rice seeds in special nursery beds fertilised with ash. The seedlings of many different varieties of rice are planted out by hand on the field ridges over several months (Fig. 81). The dykes maintain a constant depth of fresh water in the fields, and this is drained away before harvesting takes place. The soil is then turned again and a further crop planted. Some fields produce three crops per year in this way. There are no associations, successions or fallows but Fulani cattle are pastured on the rice fields during the dry season from January to May. Other crops, such as oil palm, maize, cassava, cocoyam and groundnut, are grown on drier plots. The main source of protein in the Baga diet is fish.

7

Movement and communications

Movement is a feature of life in rural Africa. Individuals travel in order to trade or visit relations and groups of people move in search of new land to cultivate or to graze, new places for their homes, more territory to occupy, or even to escape from the expansionist designs of others. The present ethnic groupings in Africa have been formed from the complex movements of people within the continent over many centuries. Two processes are common in these population movements: the merging of differing peoples to form new groups which retain fragments of the language, history and social organisation of their ancestors; and the splitting up of a unit so that over years the separate groups develop different customs and languages.

The Baga group of the Guinea coast, for instance, contain many people of diverse origins who all sought refuge from slave catchers in the coastal swamps. Now they speak the same language and cultivate the soil in the same way but they do not all build the same kind of house. One of the units within the Baga group consists of people who are thought to have come from Mopti on the Inland Niger Delta in the eighteenth century, bringing with them a particular kind of floating rice (*Oryza glaberrima*). In comparison, a group in east Africa known as the Lwoo moved away in small units from their homeland in the southern Sudan, each unit travelling at its own pace. The units inter-married with different peoples and settled down in different areas. Some retained their own language and customs while others took the language and customs of their partners. Today distinct groups such as the Alur, the Acholi and the Luo are their descendants.

Transport and trade routes

The regular movement of people and goods on a large scale was limited in the past by the difficulties involved. Walking was the traditional form of transport in forested rural Africa, and goods were carried on the head. Only small loads (Table 14) can be carried in this way and very short distances covered each day. Imperishable commodities which command a high price in comparison to their weight are the only goods which can be carried any distance by this method – gold, salt and ivory, for instance.

Table 14. The approximate loads (in kilos) various forms of animal transport can carry

Man	27
Donkey	50
Mule	67
Camel	240

In the more open vegetation and drier conditions of the savanna, donkeys, mules, oxen and camels are used as pack animals. As they can carry heavier loads (Table 14) a more elaborate and extensive trade network could develop in the savanna, covering a wide area and transporting a larger range of commodities. The wheel was not part of the traditional technology of rural tropical Africa and so carts were never made. Pathways were worn rather than constructed; obstacles were avoided rather than removed; and bridges were rare so river crossings during the wet season were frequently hazardous. Lakes, rivers and coastal lagoons made canoe and dhow travel possible. Certain kinds of social organisation had an influence on the pattern of local communications. The centralised kingdom of Buganda in the nineteenth century, for example, had an excellent system of roads which radiated out from the king's palace, and the Ashanti kingdom at the same time maintained its dominance over the surrounding country by similar means (Fig. 82).

For centuries before the colonial era there was a flourishing trade across the Sahara. North African salt, copper and cattle and European goods were exchanged for west African gold, slaves and kola nuts (Fig. 83). The detailed description of Kano market in 1851 made by the German traveller Heinrich Barth gives a good idea of the variety of products involved and the areas from which they came (Table 15).

Table 15. Imports of Kano in 1851, as described by Heinrich Barth

Source	Product	Comments
Manchester, England	Calicos	Part dyed and re-exported to Ghadames
Manchester, England	Muslins	
Saxony	Red and green woollen cloth	Going out of fashion
Solingen	Sword blades	Blades set and re-exported
Nuremberg, Bavaria	Needles and looking-glasses	Cheap
Nuremberg, Bavaria	Common paper	Used for wrapping
France	French silks	Re-exported to Yorubaland and Gonja
France	Sugar	In small loaves of 1.1 kg each
Styria	Common razors	Cheap
Venice and Trieste	Beads	Low price, reduced supply
Tunis and Egypt	Articles of Arab dress	
Egypt	White shawls	
Tripoli and Darfur	Copper and zinc	
	Silver	
	Tin	
	Gold	
	Salt	
	Frankincense and spices	
	Rose oil	Expensive, mainly for the upper classes

82 The great roads of Ashanti in the early nineteenth century

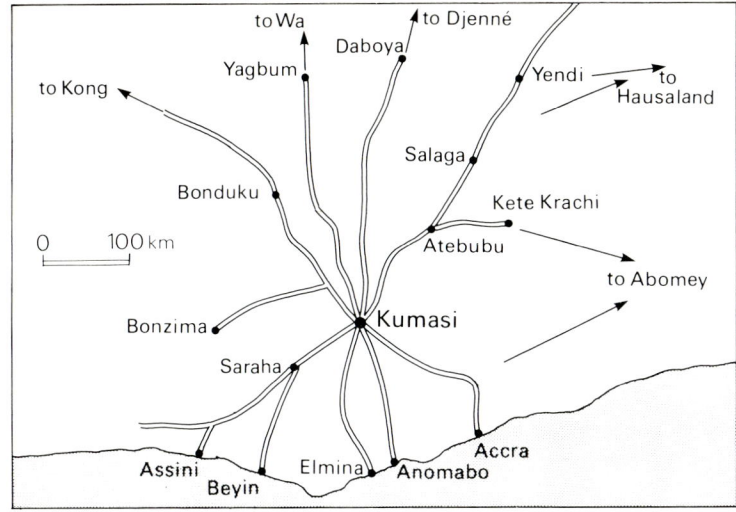

83 Trade routes in north and west Africa in the sixteenth century

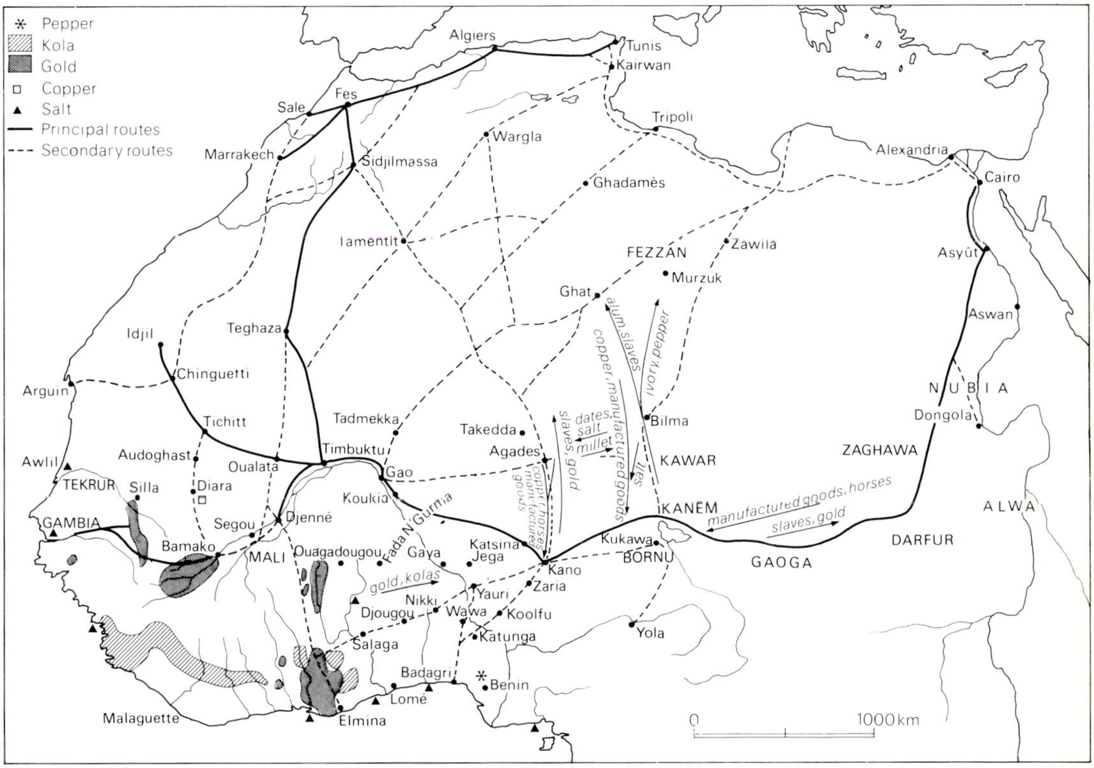

In east Africa the coastal people have been involved in sea trade with Arabia and India from Roman times. The fortunes of the coastal ports have varied over the centuries but from the contacts between Africans and Arabs emerged the Swahili language and culture. The coastal people did not venture inland before the nineteenth century but groups from the interior such as the Kamba, the Nyamwezi and the Yao brought ivory, tortoiseshell, gold, iron ore and slaves to exchange for imported cloth, beads, wire and porcelain. In the nine-

84 East African trade routes in the nineteenth century

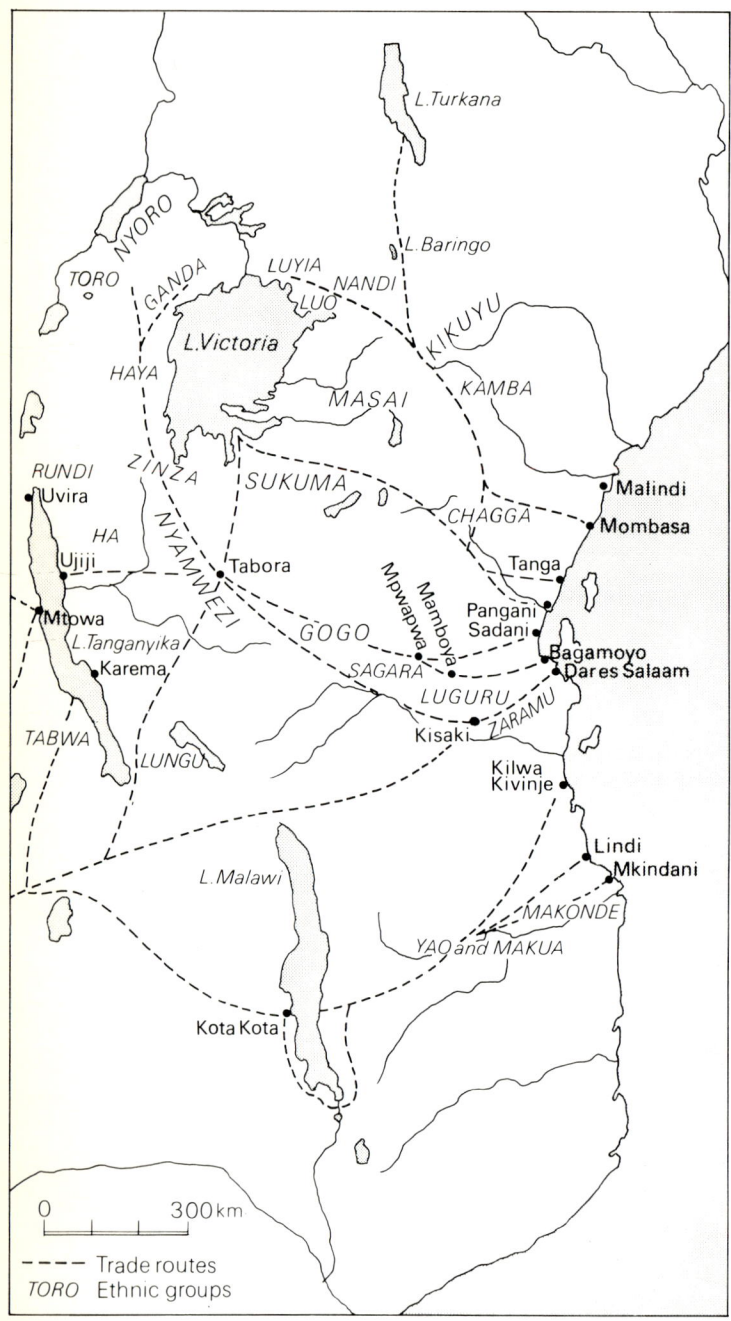

teenth century Arab caravans began to travel inland in order to obtain more regular supplies to meet the growing demand for ivory and slaves (Fig. 84).

In central Africa long-distance trade routes radiated from the copper mines of Katanga worked by the Lunda people. Most of the copper circulated within the continent and only small amounts reached the coast. Bark cloth and salt were also important in the internal trade of east and central Africa.

Table 16. Some examples of trade exchanges in east and central Africa in the nineteenth century

Group	Commodity sold	Purchaser	Exchange payment
Kikuyu	Food	Masai	Livestock
Kikuyu	Iron implements	Embu	Livestock
Kikuyu	Iron implements	Kamba	Livestock
Nyoro	Iron hoes	Teso	Ivory, hides, goats, food
Nyoro	Iron hoes	Lango	Ivory, hides, goats, food
Lango	Iron hoes	Teso	Cattle
Lango	Iron hoes	Kumam	Cattle
Masai	Hides	Chagga	Plantains
Pokomo	Food	Galla	Ivory
Pokomo	Food	Swahili	Axes, hoes
Pokomo	Food	Boma	Bows and arrows
Henga	Salt	Phoka	Hoes

There are two kinds of trade: first, networks involving specific groups of people who control the acquisition, transport and disposal of goods, carrying them long distances from areas of supply to areas of demand; and, second, a relay trade. The latter is the exchange of goods between groups of people living close to one another. The goods may travel over wide areas, albeit slowly, with many people handling them en route. Some examples of the kind of exchanges which took place in east Africa are listed in Table 16.

The orientation of the trade and communications network began to change in response to the interest of European states in tropical Africa, which dates from the sixteenth century, and to the development of transport technology, which took place in the nineteenth and twentieth centuries. The initial major interest of the Europeans in Africa was slaves but after the abolition of the slave trade in the nineteenth century tropical crops and minerals became the chief concern. As the Europeans came to Africa by sea the primary points of contact were the ports, which became the nodes of new communications networks. The old networks of paths were replaced by railways, roads and air routes. In rural areas, however, paths are still very important.

In east Africa, where coastal trade had always been important, European contact and penetration of the interior followed a pre-existing pattern. In west Africa, however, where the Atlantic coast had been an unimportant backwater of the Saharan network, European interest stimulated a change in orientation. Coastal towns developed at the expense of the great trading towns such as Timbuktu and Gao on the edge of the Sahara.

The boundaries of most of the modern states were fixed during the colonial period and the new forms of communication were organised within these boundaries. Railways were still the leading mode of transport at the end of the nineteenth century and the colonial administrations built limited networks in most of their

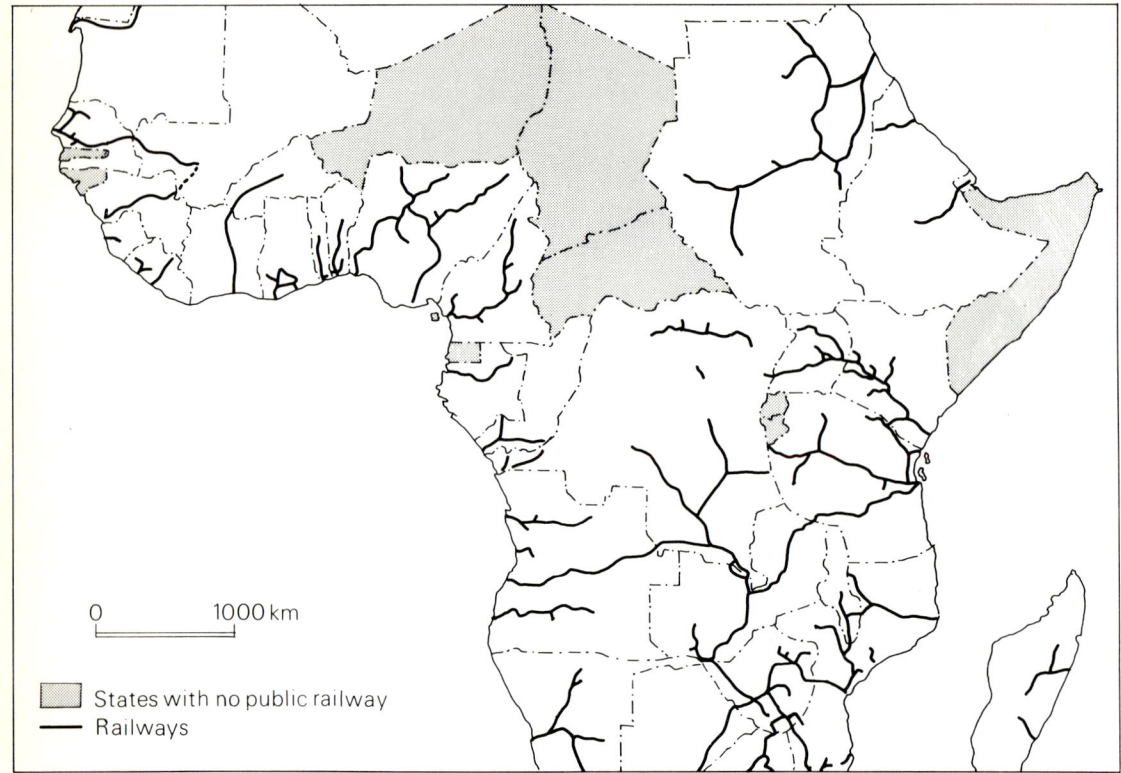

85 Railway lines in tropical Africa

possessions to extend their control and to facilitate the export of crops and minerals (Fig. 85). The selection of particular ports as termini of rail networks gave them a major advantage over other ports, which subsequently declined. Ghana, for instance, had thirty ports along its 500 km of coast in 1900 but only Sekondi-Takoradi and Accra-Tema are important today.

As motor transport increased in importance, roads were built as feeders to the railways and subsequently independent networks were established. By no means all roads in Africa are bitumenised today. Many are made of laterite, an iron-rich stoney material, or simply compacted earth, and are impassable in the wet season. Under the tropical climatic conditions road surfaces disintegrate rapidly and construction and maintenance costs are very high. The creation of a network of motorable roads, however, has a profound effect on the direction of movement of produce. For instance, the movement of the cocoa crop from the Ondo area of Nigeria to the port of Lagos has followed three routes this century (Fig. 86), depending on their quality and availability at any one time. Motor road networks also influence the fortunes of settlements. An example was the building of a motor road across the Tano River at Acherensua in the Ahafo area of Ghana. It bypassed the original focus of Ahafo settlement at Sienchem and stimulated the rise of Goaso as the present administrative centre (Fig. 87). The old trading town of Jega in Nigeria, formerly comparable with Kano, was bypassed by modern roads and has declined into insignificance.

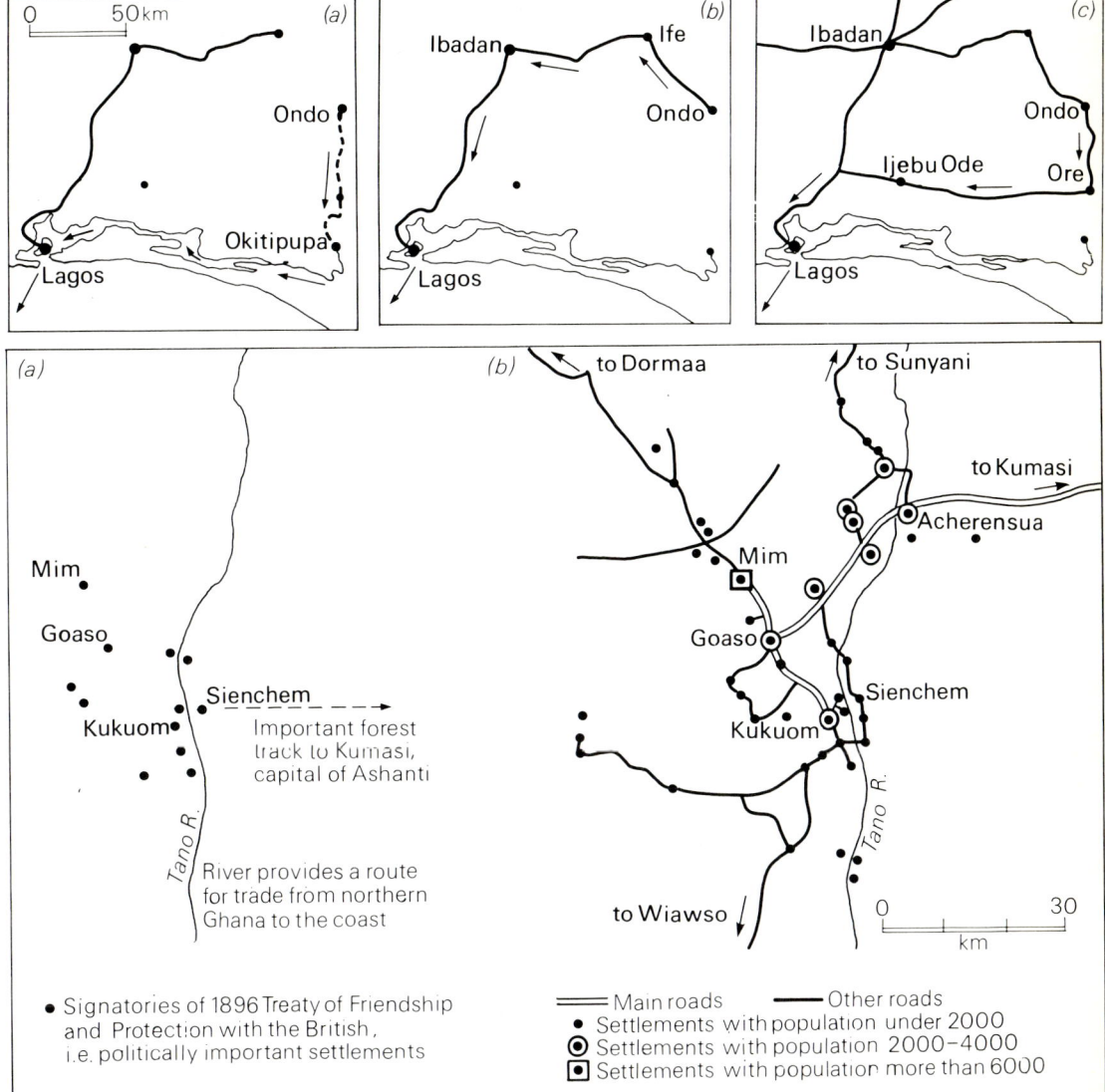

86 Changing routes for the export of cocoa from Ondo, Nigeria
The dates are approximations only
a. Pre-1950 (road to Okitipupa, then water to Lagos); b. post-1950 (Ondo-Ife road tarred); c. post-1964 (Ijebu-Benin motorway)

87 Changes in accessibility in Ahafo
a. The original focus of Ahafo settlement;
b. present-day communications and settlement size in Ahafo

Most rural people cannot afford to own vehicles but public transport is popular. The usual kind in rural areas, providing the cheapest ride, is the covered lorry with plank seats and plenty of space for loads, the west African mammy waggon. Other, more expensive forms are minibuses and taxis. Paths remain the only links between many villages; the bicycle is particularly popular and has made a significant impact in densely populated areas such as Iboland in Nigeria and Buganda in Uganda.

Taaffe, Morrill and Gould have described a model of the stages of growth of a communications network in a developing country which Hoyle has applied to east Africa (Figs. 88, 89). The pre-colonial network is virtually ignored and no distinction is made between the different modes of transport and their various requirements. A model which could incorporate paths, cycle tracks, different road surfaces,

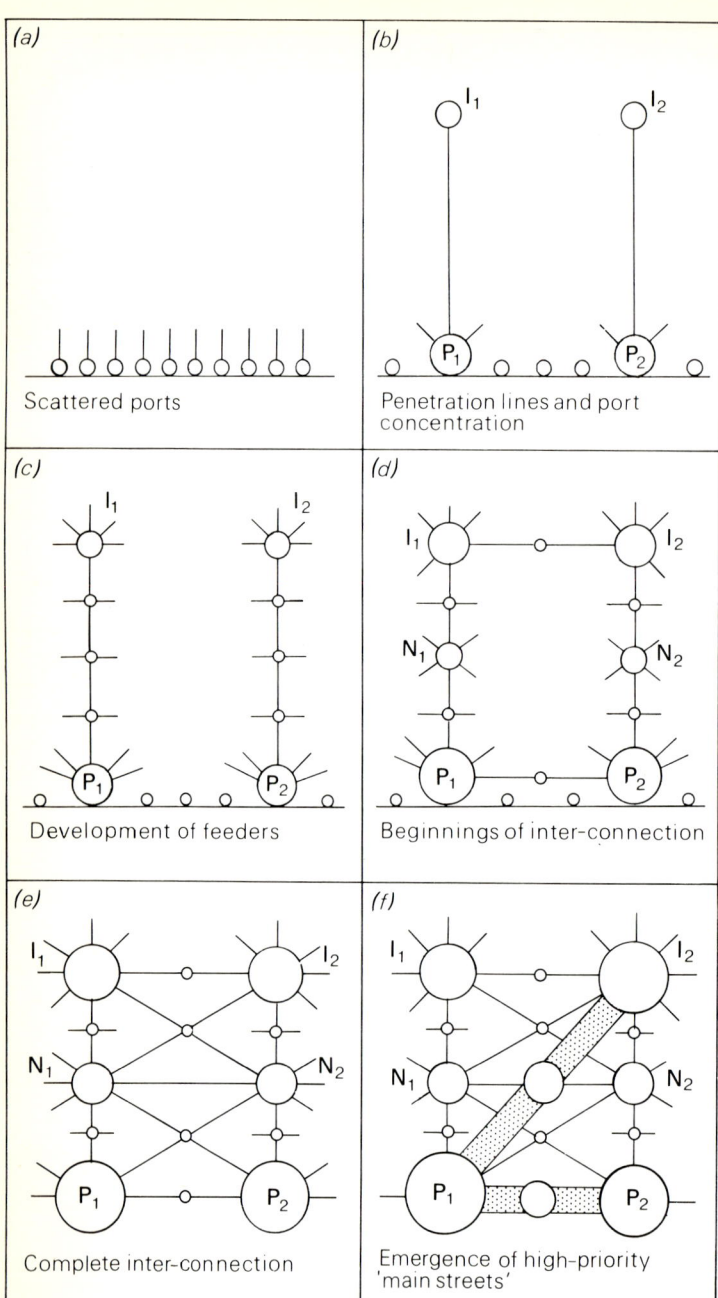

88 A model sequence of transport development by Taaffe, Morrill and Gould

railways, waterways and airlines and take into account whether they functioned throughout the year would be most useful. The model shown in Fig. 88 makes clear-cut divisions between stages which are not apparent in reality and, as the authors stress, several stages may be taking place simultaneously in different sections of one network. Lateral 'inter-connections' may be taking place close to the original 'penetration lines' while new 'penetration lines' are extending the network on the periphery. In Africa the 'high-priority "main streets"' usually follow one of the original 'penetration lines' rather than breaking new ground, as urban and industrial growth tends to concentrate in the areas which gained an initial advantage in transport matters. Lack of good communications is still a big problem in

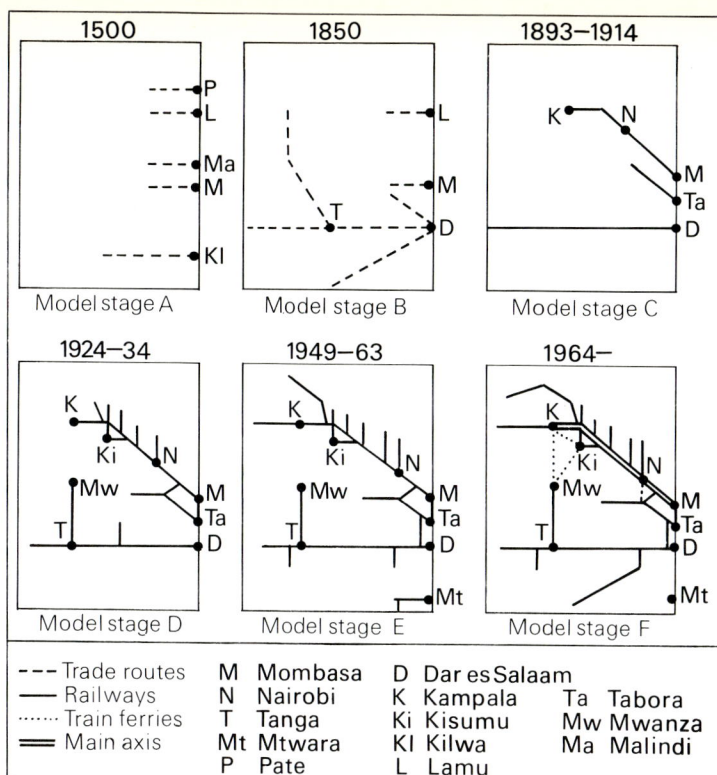

89 An application of the Taaffe, Morrill and Gould model of transport development in east Africa, by Hoyle

most parts of rural Africa but the costs of construction, the vast areas involved and the small size of most of the individual economies ensure that improvements can be made only slowly.

Both internal and external trade have benefited from the improvements which have been made in communications. Groundnuts were not a significant export of Nigeria until after the railway reached Kano in 1912; Kenya now exports soft fruits and fresh flowers by air to the luxury markets of Europe. Much of the export trade is with the developed world rather than other African countries. This is a result of the colonial period when African economies were encouraged to supply primary produce to Europe and to provide in turn a market for European manufactured goods. The major operators in the export trade today are marketing boards, co-operative societies and European firms. After sale by the producer, goods pass through the hands of several middlemen, who deal in progressively larger quantities before reaching the exporting body. The retailing of imported goods follows a similar pattern in the reverse direction, with many intermediaries reducing the size of the units sold (Table 17). As the purchasing power in rural areas is low, local retailers sell such things as cigarettes, matches and sugar lumps singly.

Table 17. Distributive system for imported goods

1 Importing company	Reduction
2 Wholesale dealer	in
3 Storekeeper	size
4 Market stallholder	of
5 Small street stallholder	unit
6 Hawker	↓ sold

Markets and marketing

Markets are a feature of modern rural African life (Fig. 90). In east and central Africa markets were not important historically since most trade was carried out by individual exchange. There were exceptions, however, such as the large open market at Raba Kaya near Mombasa and the Kisi pottery market held at Pupangandu at the north end of Lake Malawi. The population has increased during the twentieth century, and there has been an increase in commercial activity. The location and availability of modern markets in east and central Africa depend on the size and distribution of the population and its purchasing power. These markets are generally held on a weekly basis. In west Africa markets have a much longer history and demonstrate some interesting locational principles. Markets are frequently held in settlements but some take place on isolated sites. The Saturday market at Makɔkou in Gabon, for instance, attracts many people from surrounding villages but the place itself is inhabited during the week only by civil servants and European merchants. In Yorubaland there are market sites at path intersections where no one at all lives.

Markets have several functions: they provide opportunities for people to sell their produce, to purchase necessities and luxuries, to meet friends, business associates, political allies, to obtain services such as letter-writing and gold smithing, and for entertainment. Among the Tiv the social functions of the market are considered to be quite as important as the economic functions. For each Tiv sub-group the five days of the Tiv week are named after the sites of the five local markets which take place in succession; thus the markets provide a time reference for the people.

The main economic function of rural African markets is the sale of local agricultural produce to buyers who amass a bulk stock for re-sale elsewhere. Much of this bulked produce goes directly from the rural to the urban areas; some goes to areas of commercial cropping where there is a demand for extra foodstuffs but in general

90 A scene in a large market in Mali with onions for sale in the foreground, rice and other grain behind

Table 18. Changes in Aveyime market, Lower Volta, Ghana, 1954–64

	1954	1964
Frequency	Seasonal, twice weekly	All year, twice weekly
Range of number of sellers per day	50–700	270–850
Average number of sellers per day	180	500
Number of lorries visiting market per day	3–10 (0 in rainy season)	40–50
Goods and services for sale:		
a. Local foodstuffs	29 items	43 items
b. Imported foods	0	10 items
c. Other imported goods	1 cloth trader (occasionally) 1–2 Hausa haberdashery traders	40–50 cloth traders 8 Hausa haberdashery traders 3 cooked-meat sellers
d. Locally manufactured goods	Small quantity shea-butter and soap	10 items
e. Craftsmen	1 blacksmith 3 tailors 1 seamstress	5 blacksmiths 3 tailors 2 seamstresses 4 goldsmiths 3 carpenters 1 shoemaker 1 fitter
f. Other businesses	1 letter-writer 2 chop (food) bars 3 licensed bars 1 stationery stall	1 letter-writer 3 chop bars 5 licensed bars 5 corn mills 2 kerosene/petrol-sellers 1 petrol-seller

trade between rural areas is much less important. The bulk buyers come from the urban areas to purchase the agricultural produce, whereas the trade between rural areas is operated by local village traders. The main items of trade between rural areas are fish from the coast and the Inland Niger Delta, salt, palm oil, kola nuts and cattle, while in Nigeria yams and rice are also important commodities. Improved accessibility can stimulate the growth of a market as can be seen in Table 18. Aveyime market increased in size as a result of the construction of an all-weather road and a new market place and lorry park. The growth of a market's size stimulates an increase in the amount of retail trade and a greater diversity in the items offered for sale. Retail trade consists of some unprocessed local foodstuffs for those members of the rural population such as teachers who are unable to grow all their requirements, cooked foodstuffs, a little produce from other rural areas, craft objects such as

91 Market periodicities in west Africa

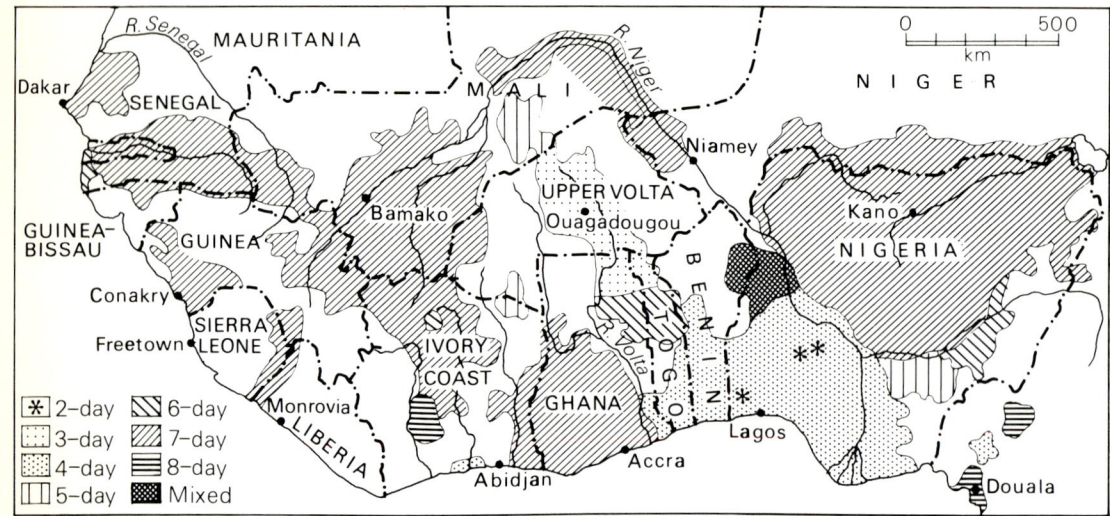

mats and baskets and imported or manufactured goods from the towns. Shops are uncommon in rural areas since demand is very limited. Those that do exist frequently open only on market days, with their owner engaging in farming the rest of the time.

In towns there are daily markets selling foodstuffs but the rural markets normally take place at intervals of several days. The length of time between successive markets at a particular site varies with the area. In Ghana and southern Mali the interval is seven days and in southern Nigeria it is four (Fig. 91). The interval may be a reflection of the purchasing power and the frequency of the need to buy and sell in an area or it may be linked to the traditional, colonial or Islamic ideas about the organisation of time. Not enough is known about the history of these periodic markets to be precise about why they occur when they do. In some areas markets form part of a cycle, so that in one locality there is a market each day but at a different site (Fig. 92). Markets occurring on the same day are in direct competition with one another and are usually further apart than markets within the cycle occurring on different days. By taking place at different sites on different days a cycle of periodic markets can draw on a larger population of produce sellers and consumers than a single fixed market can. The convenience of the consumers and produce sellers seems to be more important than the distance traders have to cover. Many traders visit only selected markets and return to their own homes every evening. The activities which one normally accepts as taking place at fixed points, central places, shift from one place to another in a regular cyclic fashion.

In some areas such as Tivland the individual market cycles overlap so that a market may appear in two cycles (Fig. 93). In this way goods and information can travel from one circuit to another. Although Tiv markets are very important as social events they also provide a range of economic activities. In most markets women sell vegetables, spices and other ingredients for household cooking. In larger markets both men and women sell agricultural goods and craft articles to produce buyers. In the major markets, which are few, there are dealers who buy goods cheaply and take them to other

92 Periodic markets in western Nigeria in 1967

93 Overlapping market cycles in southern Tivland, Nigeria

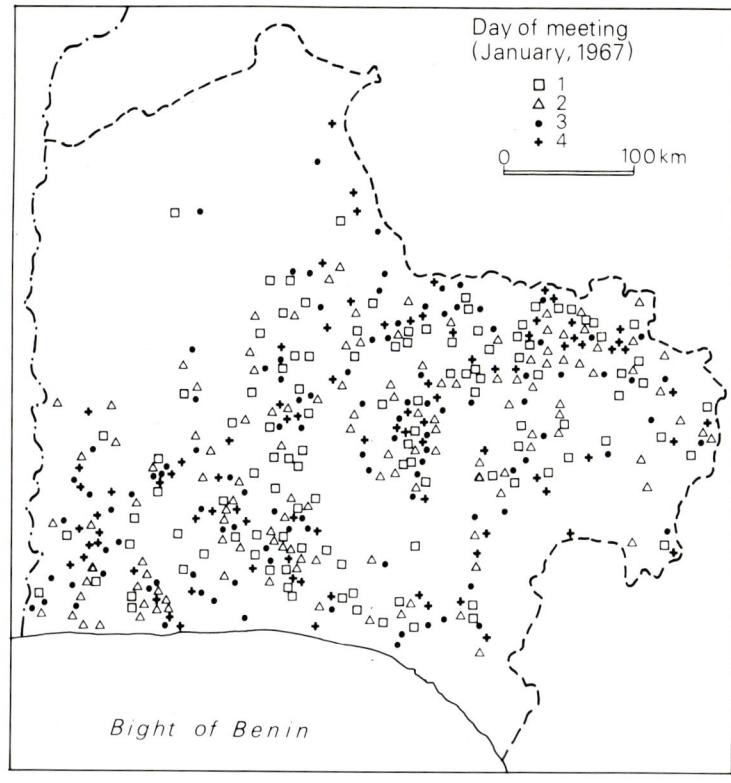

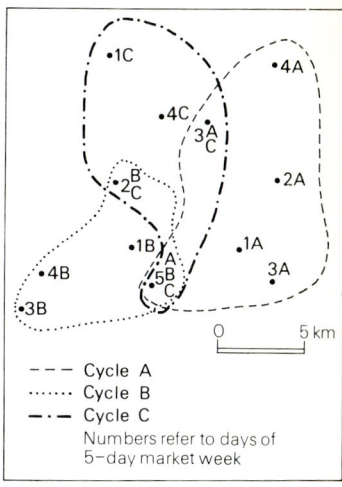

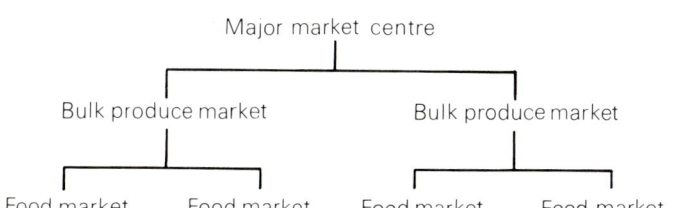

94 The functional hierarchy of Tiv markets

areas where they will fetch a good price. These varying market activities can be arranged in a functional hierarchy (Fig. 94).

Trading

Although markets exist in Hausaland, a large proportion of trade does not take place in the market place. Married Hausa women, who maintain the Islamic tradition of purdah — seclusion of women — and rarely leave their houses, supply grain and cooked foods to purchasers, using old women and children as intermediaries. A great deal of the Hausa long-distance trade also operates from houses. The principal organisers are landlords who provide accommodation for dealers in Hausa localities all over west Africa. The major participants are usually town dwellers but the trade involves many rural people as well. For instance, in the kola trade in western Nigeria, Hausa guides and brokers live near the Yoruba kola farmers and effect sales between them and the town-based Hausa traders (Fig. 95). The Hausa landlords perform many roles (Table 19), and the cohesion of

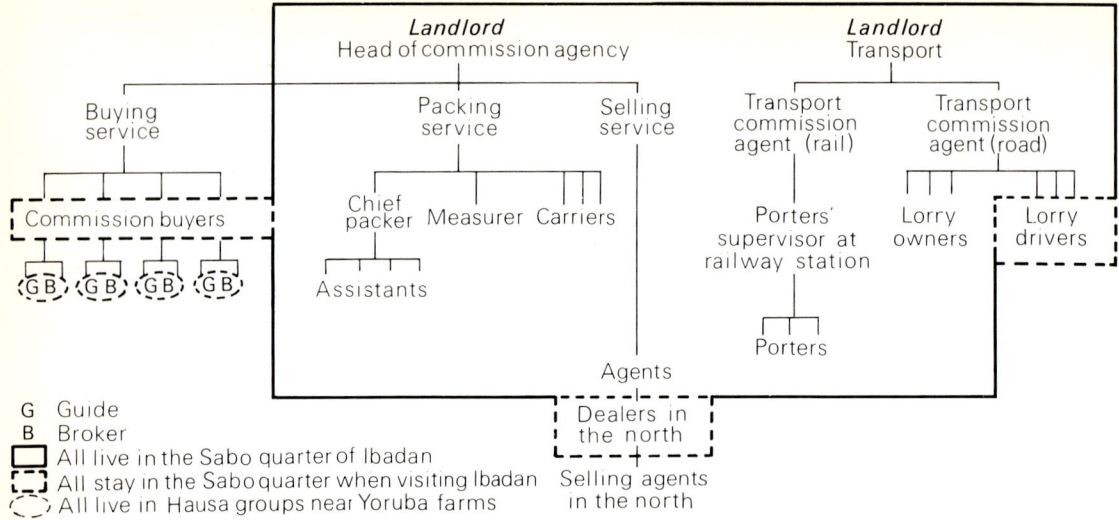

95 The organisation and residence of Hausa kola traders in Nigeria

Table 19. Possible roles of a Hausa landlord

1 Provider of accommodation for dealers
2 Broker, introducing dealers to producers and purchasers
3 Dealer in own right
4 Organiser of transport of produce
5 Monetary adviser to dealers
6 Grantor or guarantor of credit
7 Wholesaler, providing storage facilities for produce

the system is based on the fact that the participants all live close to each other in such places as the Sabo area of Ibadan and the Zongo area of Kumasi.

The Hausa engage in trade mainly in the dry season, when agricultural activity is severely limited. The Hausa of the Katsina area of Nigeria, for instance, take tobacco north to Zinder and Agadès in Niger and return with cattle and natron (sodium sesquicarbonate, a salt used for soups and needed by livestock as a 'cattle-lick'), which they take south to Ibadan and Abeokuta where they purchase kola nuts to take home to Katsina. About two-thirds of the live cattle trade in Nigeria is carried by rail but about a third of the cattle involved are walked, frequently accompanied by Fulani herdsmen, from the producing areas in the north to the markets of the south. Cattle carried by rail fetch a higher price than the 'foot cattle' and can be kept in Ibadan for up to two and a half months before slaughter. The 'foot cattle' suffer from the physical strain of the long walk, which could be over 1500 km, and the high risk of contracting trypanosomiasis en route, so they have to be slaughtered within two weeks of their arrival in the south. Some cattle are sold off at specialised cattle markets in places on the way such as Ilorin, Ogbomosho and Oyo (Fig. 96), although usually they fetch a lower price than they would further south. In Ghana the cattle trade of Kumasi draws on two sources of supply. Animals from Upper Volta and Mali dominate the trade from September to April while stock from northern Ghana is sold in the intervening season, when both demand and prices are high.

Foreigners, either non-nationals of the states concerned or non-Africans, have frequently played significant roles in trade in tropical

96 Cattle routes in Nigeria

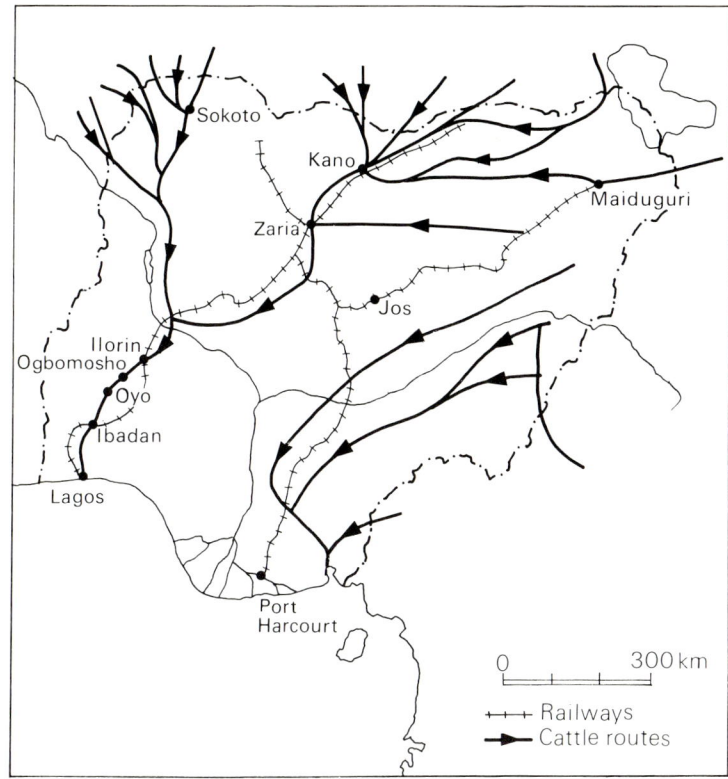

African countries. The Hausa and Dioula are both mobile groups of people trading all over west Africa, and the Yoruba from Nigeria formed a significant trading community in Ghana until the Ghanaian government introduced residence permits for non-nationals in the Aliens Decree of 1969. The Lebanese are a small but important commercial community in west Africa and people from the subcontinent of India figure prominently in east and central Africa. There, people of Asian origin run village stores, factories for processing foodstuffs, some plantations and much local transport, although many Asians with British citizenship were expelled from Uganda in 1971. In Madagascar, where the population has a strong Indonesian element in its composition, the commercial community contains both Indians and Chinese.

Religion

Trade goods are not the only items which are mobile in rural areas. Ideas, innovations and facilities permeate societies and alter attitudes, technologies and standards of living. Often this kind of movement was linked in the past with the actual movements of groups of people and the imposition of alien rule. The spread of the Muslim religion and the associated Arabic culture, language, writing, legal and educational systems is linked with military efforts. The conquest of the area north of Senegal and Niger rivers by Arab peoples before the eighteenth century led to the forcible conversion of most of the local inhabitants to Islam and the establishment of Islamic centres of learning at Djenné and Timbuktu. Later, energetic new African converts fought holy wars, called *jihads*, to further the interests of their religion. Notable among these was the Fulani, Usuman dan Fodio, who attacked and conquered the Hausa states as well as part of the Nupe and Yoruba areas from 1804 to 1810. Fulani leaders, called Emirs, were placed in charge of the conquered peoples and Muslim states were established. The success of this enterprise stimulated further Fulani *jihads* in other parts of west Africa. In east Africa, Islam was brought to the coastal area by the Arab traders but missionary activity was slight and there was little penetration inland. Later on the settlement of communities of Asians, some of whom were Muslims, established the Islamic religion in the interior of east Africa. A number of different Muslim sects are represented in these Asian communities and the number of local converts is small. Fig. 97 illustrates the extent of the Muslim influence in Africa today.

As one might expect, Christianity spread in Africa along the lines of European penetration. In some areas the Christian missionaries arrived before the colonial administrators and they were frequently instrumental in setting up health and educational facilities as well as in teaching their faith. The variety of sects of the Christian religion found elsewhere in the world are represented in Africa. Some groups of people, such as the Ibo in Nigeria and the Ganda in Uganda, have been attracted to world-wide sects of Christianity in large numbers, but in many areas local Christian churches, which express the religion through African culture, have developed and attract many adherents.

Services

Medical facilities were some of the earliest 'modern' features to reach the rural areas. Gould suggests that roads and dispensaries, for instance, were the first aspects of 'the modernisation process' to appear in Tanzania during the 1920s. In rural areas, modern medical facilities generally consist of dispensaries and maternity centres, although some areas do have health centres and even small hospitals. Most highly qualified personnel such as doctors prefer to live and work in towns rather than villages. Patients with acute health problems, therefore, still have to travel considerable distances to towns for assistance and treatment. In some countries, notably Kenya and Zambia, a 'Flying Doctor' service has been introduced to cope with the problems of distance and a widely scattered population.

Primary-level educational facilities, which are frequently associated with Christian missionary activity, are very common in rural Africa, particularly in the non-Muslim countries. In Islamic areas the usual form of schooling is the Koranic school. Primary education for all has not yet been attained in tropical Africa as it is expensive to provide and requires much skilled manpower, which so far is not available. Secondary schools and higher educational facilities are rarely found in rural areas and can be considered a feature of the urban African scene.

The provision of expensive facilities such as electricity, piped water supplies and telephones, which are costly to install and run, are more common in towns than country areas and they are penetrating the rural scene very slowly. Usually only highly paid salary earners such as civil servants, teachers or mining personnel can afford

97 The significance of the Muslim religion in tropical Africa

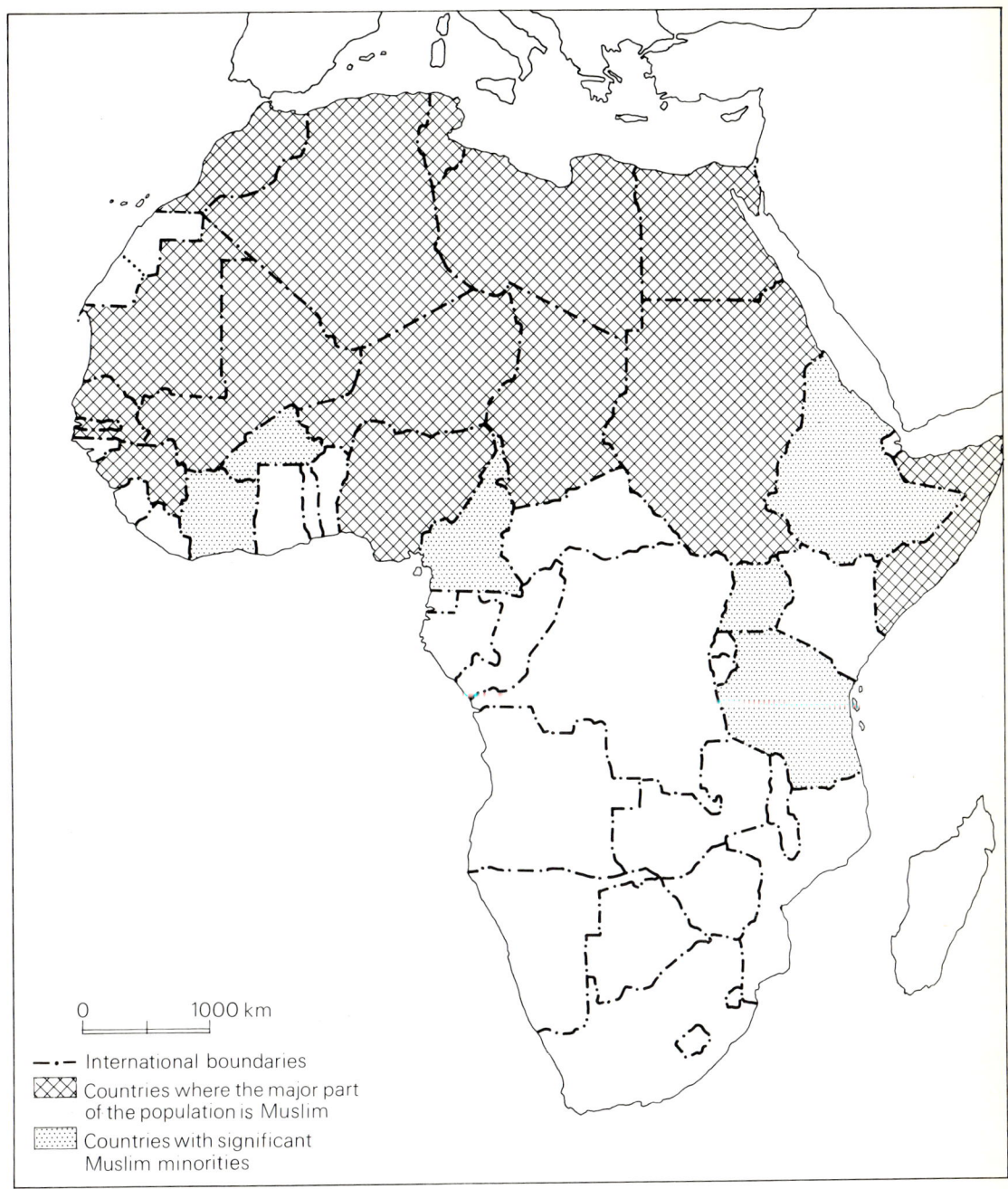

- — · — International boundaries
- ⊠ Countries where the major part of the population is Muslim
- ▒ Countries with significant Muslim minorities

these facilities if they are in fact available at all in the rural areas. The radio is a very important method of spreading information in country districts, where it supplements the traditional method of communication, the drum. Radios are not too expensive to buy or run and they provide both instruction and entertainment.

Service facilities in rural areas tend to be concentrated in particular localities creating nodes of development, even in areas of dispersed

115

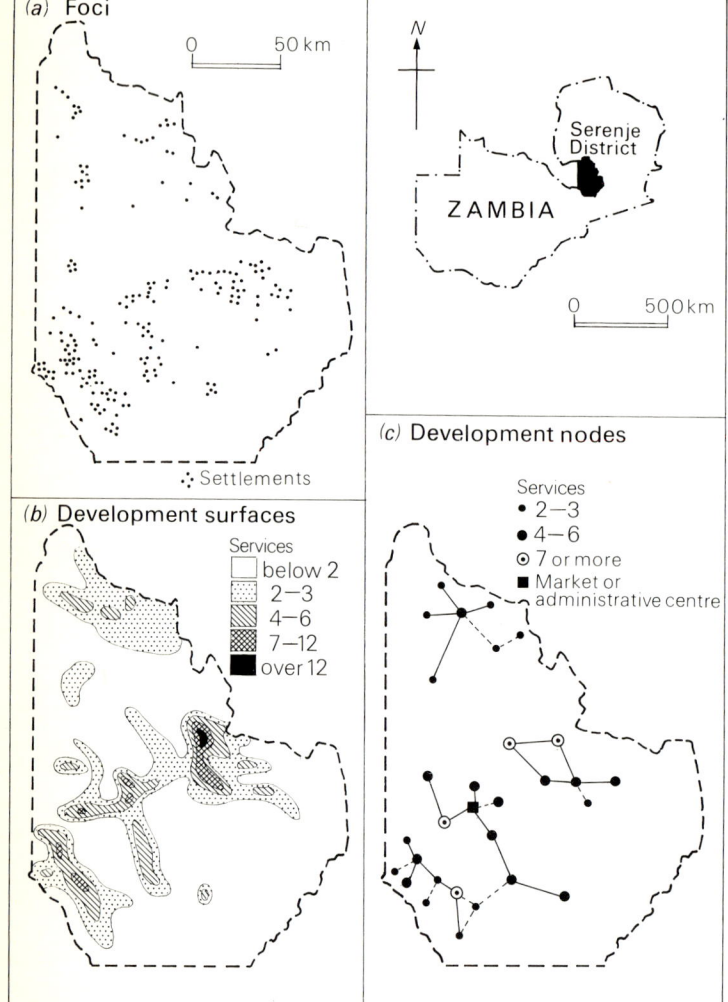

98 Rural service development in the Serenje district of Zambia
The rural services include a rural shop, women's development group, farm co-operative, community development project, agricultural demonstrator, radio farm forum group, primary school clinic, grinding mill, and tractor (either private or government). A development surface or node of a particular value denotes the number of rural services available in that locality

population (Fig. 98). This is especially true of institutions like banks and agricultural credit organisations, which are important in assisting and promoting the growth of agricultural production. Many innovations spread into rural areas from the towns and diffuse through a hierarchy. In such cases the presence of lines of communication and centres of population is important in speeding up the diffusion process. Large concentrated villages with road links to near-by towns provide more opportunities for rural people to come in contact with new ideas than do small dispersed homesteads (Fig. 99). Some innovations which are more relevant to people living in the country than people living in the towns, such as the co-operative societies for selling agricultural produce, spread in a more contagious fashion through a population. In Sierra Leone the establishment of co-operative societies in certain areas provided models for their development in neighbouring areas, particularly as the early societies were immediate successes and brought noticeable monetary benefits to the participants.

99 'Hierarchical' and 'contagious' diffusion of services in Sierra Leone

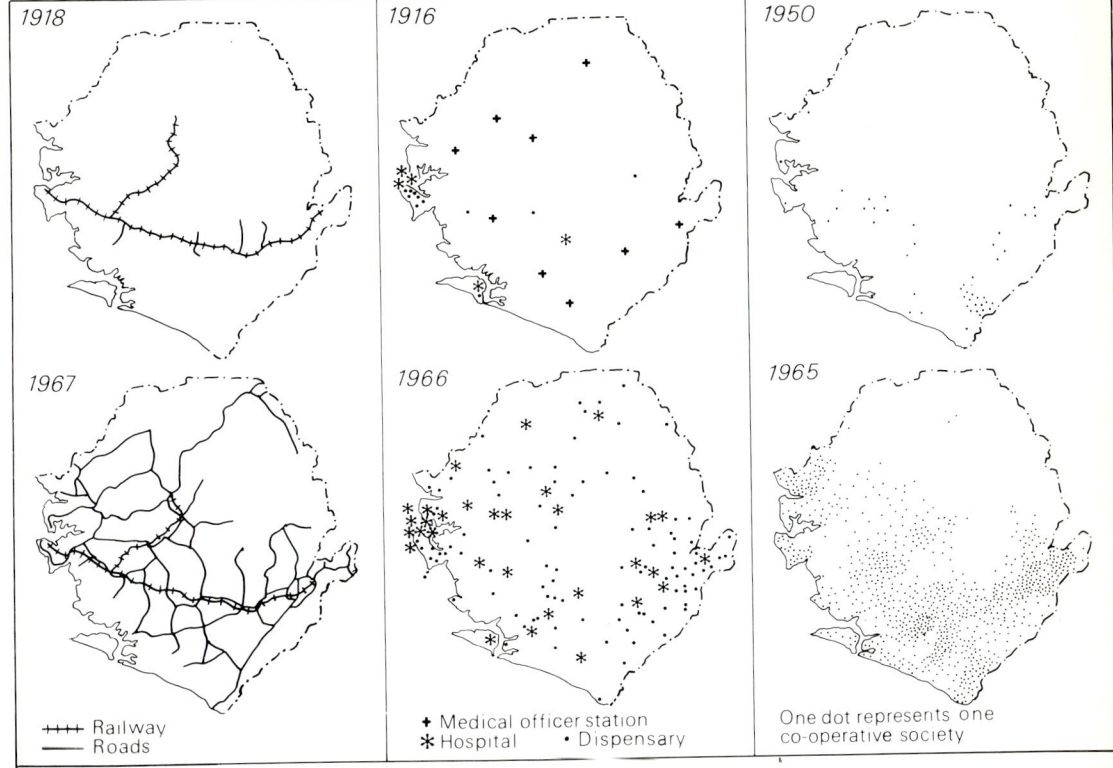

Movements of people

The mobility of the population is a significant feature of rural life in tropical Africa. People do not travel only because they are fishermen, nomadic herdsmen, shifting cultivators or traders, but for many other reasons. A recent survey of people travelling on public transport in some parts of west Africa showed that over 40% were making journeys of a social nature, to attend family functions or to visit relations and friends. Each year many Muslims make the long pilgrimage to the sacred city of Mecca in Saudi Arabia. The wealthy pilgrims travel by air but a considerable number journey overland from west Africa, taking several years over the expedition and often working for a while in the Republic of the Sudan en route. In some areas there have been movements by refugees from political changes and troubles. Uganda, for instance, has a large population of refugees from Rwanda, Burundi and the southern Sudan. In contrast to this there have also been movements of people from defensive to more accessible sites with the establishment of stable political order. This movement is often over short distances, such as the change in location of the village of Idanre in western Nigeria from the top of a steep-sided inselberg to the foot.

Governments are frequently instrumental in the movement of people. In Africa many people have had to be re-settled as a result of hydro-electric power schemes which have necessitated the creation of large lakes, flooding many villages. In the Sudan Republic people from Wadi Halfa affected by the enlargement of the Aswan Dam and

Lake Nasser were re-settled on the Khashm el Girba scheme mentioned in Chapter 5. Movements of this kind are disruptive and alter considerably the social organisation, agricultural practices and economies of the people involved. On a smaller scale there are movements of people onto special agricultural settlement schemes like the Mwea scheme in Kenya mentioned in Chapter 4 or tsetse fly control schemes such as the Anchau settlement in northern Nigeria. In Tanzania the government has an ambitious scheme to concentrate the scattered rural population into villages known as *ujamaa* villages, which are intended to operate on a self-help co-operative basis and also be large enough to receive services at an economic cost.

One final set of population movements is that of people looking for employment. In west Africa many people from the savanna areas still migrate seasonally. During the dry season they move to areas further south where they find work helping with the cocoa and groundnut harvests. Others go to work for longer periods on plantations or move to the towns. In the rest of tropical Africa the people tend to stay away from home for one or two years and to work in urban or industrial areas. In southern Africa this movement is more organised as mining employers recruit the labour force they require in the rural areas. Supply and demand for labour are affected by elements of attraction and deterrence which are called 'push-and-pull' factors and are elaborated in Table 20. Many rural dwellers have to move to urban areas at some time in their life for education, training, health facilities or employment and hence the rural and urban environments are inter-related. Foodstuffs from the rural areas are needed in increasing amounts to feed the growing urban populations while finance and research into agricultural development tend to come from town-based organisations. The life styles of the rural and urban populations differ considerably and in many areas the gulf between rich and poor is increasing. This is equally true at the country level where countries with particularly valuable resources, such as Nigeria with her oil, are able to earn large balance-of-payment surpluses which can be used for national development projects, while other countries require vast amounts of aid from the 'developed world'.

Table 20. Supply and demand for rural labour; the 'push-and-pull' factors in the South African situation

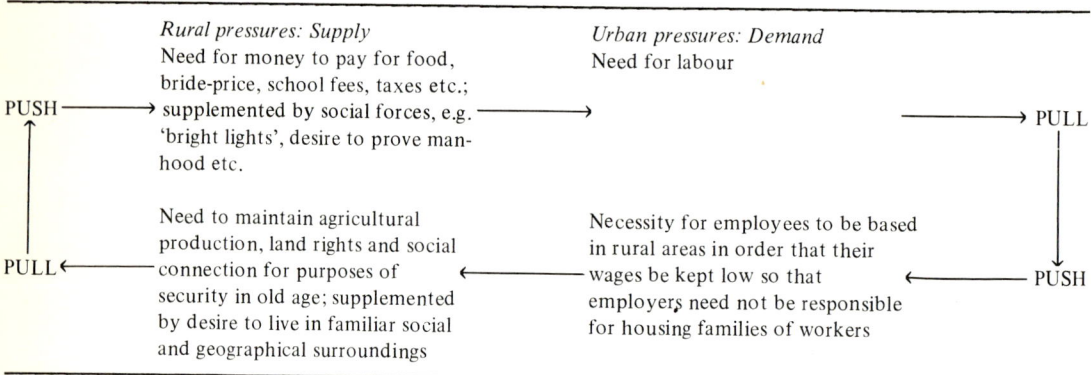

Conclusion

Rural Africa can be compared with rural areas all over the world in that all of them have experienced a lesser degree of change over the years than have their urban counterparts. Rural Africa, however, is dominated by a general level of poverty which contrasts sharply with rural Europe or North America and also with some African urban areas. There are islands of relative rural prosperity but even these would be considered poor by the farmers of the 'developed world'. But although rural Africans are poor this should not be taken to imply that they are constantly miserable and unhappy. They cope with the problem of making a living from an often difficult environment with fortitude, humour and good sense. There is, as yet, no great problem of pressure of population on the land, which is found so frequently in Asia.

With the spread of schooling, opportunities for employment at an appropriate level are very limited in the rural areas. Hence, the young and enterprising educated people are deserting the countryside to find employment and higher standards of living in the towns, leaving the land to the old, infirm or very young. This loss of manpower leads to declining agricultural standards since the maintenance of many sound, traditional, farming techniques is difficult without the assistance of able-bodied adults. Although there is tremendous variety of life styles among the ethnic groups there is also a very marked contrast between the majority of poor rural subsistence farmers and the minority of wealthy educated urban elites.

In contrast with Europe or North America the rural population of Africa depends very little on petrol, electricity or energy supplies in general. It can be argued that given the heavy exploitation of the world's resources of fossil fuels, the rural African societies with their present limited requirements are in a better position than the apparently successful advanced technologies based on a high consumption of fossil energy. They can either exploit new developments in fuel technology or just continue to survive using traditional methods. On the other hand, the current growth in urban centres presents a tremendous need for rural areas to increase the production of cheap food surplus to their own requirements. This need is particularly apparent in places like Zambia, for instance, when the funds for food at the disposal of the townspeople are reduced because of fluctuations in the world price of copper.

The effective development of the rural areas is one of the most difficult tasks facing African governments and international agencies. Very often the rural people themselves are in the best position to judge what changes would be to their advantage, but their views often have little influence on those who take the decisions. The authors hope that this book will do a little towards improving understanding of the variety of rural societies in tropical Africa and the lives and motivations of the people who live there under conditions highly dependent on the vagaries of the environment.

FURTHER READING LIST

The tropical African environment, land use and farming systems

William Allan. *The African husbandman*. Oliver and Boyd, London and Edinburgh, 1965.

J.C. de Wilde. *Experiences with agricultural development in tropical Africa*, vols. I and II. Johns Hopkins Press for the International Bank for Reconstruction and Development, Baltimore, 1967.

J.F. Griffiths, ed. *Climates of Africa*. Elsevier, Amsterdam, 1972.

B. Hopkins. *Forest and savanna. An introduction to tropical plant ecology with special reference to west Africa*. Heinemann, Ibadan and London, 1965.

P.F.M. McLoughlin, ed. *African food production systems. Cases and theory*. Johns Hopkins Press, Baltimore and London, 1970.

R. Moss. *The soil resources of tropical Africa*. Cambridge University Press, 1968.

Paul Richards, ed. *African environment: problems and perspectives*. International African Institute, London, 1975.

Hans Ruthenberg. *Farming systems in the tropics*. Oxford University Press, 1971.

M.F. Thomas and G.W. Whittington, eds. *Environment and land use in Africa*. Methuen, London, 1969.

Systematic topics

P. Bohannan and G. Dalton, eds. *Markets in Africa*. Northwestern University Press, Evanston, 1962.

J.C. Caldwell and C. Okonjo, eds. *The population of tropical Africa*. Longmans, London, 1968.

Robert Chambers. *Settlement schemes in tropical Africa. A study of organisation and development*. Routledge and Kegan Paul, London. 1969.

James L. Gibbs, ed. *Peoples of Africa*. Holt, Rinehart and Winston, New York and London, 1965.

Paul Oliver, ed. *Shelter in Africa*. Praegar, New York, 1971.

R.M. Prothero, ed. *People and land in Africa south of the Sahara. Readings in social geography*. Oxford University Press, 1972.

Elliott P. Skinner, ed. *Peoples and cultures of Africa*. The Doubleday/Natural History Press for the American Museum of Natural History, New York, 1973.

C. Turnbull. *Man in Africa*. David and Charles, Newton Abbott, 1976.

University of Edinburgh, Centre of African Studies. *Transport in Africa*. Edinburgh, 1970.

Regional material

K. Barbour. *The republic of the Sudan. A regional geography*. University of London Press, 1961.

J.I. Clarke, R.J. Harrison Church, H.R.J. Davies, D. Hilling, J. Kenworthy, D.N. McMaster, J.H. Stevens, M.B. Thorp, and H. Turay. *An advanced geography of Africa*. Hulton Educational Publications, Amersham, 1975.

D.H. Davies, ed. *Zambia in maps*. University of London Press, 1970.

A.T. Grove. *Africa*. Oxford University Press, 1978.

H.P. Huffnagel. *Agriculture in Ethiopia*. FAO, Rome, 1961.

G. Kay. *Rhodesia: a human geography*. University of London Press, 1970.

Marvin Miracle. *Agriculture in the Congo Basin: tradition and change in African rural economies*. University of Wisconsin Press, Madison, 1967.

W.B. Morgan and J.C. Pugh. *West Africa*. Methuen, London, 1969.

W.T.W. Morgan. *East Africa*. Longman, London, 1973.

Harold D. Nelson *et al. Area handbook for the United Republic of Cameroon*. Foreign Area Studies, The American University, Washington, 1974.

S.H. Ominde, ed. *Studies in east African geography and development*. Heinemann, London, 1970.

J.G. Pike and G.T. Rimmington. *Malawi: a geographical study*. Oxford University Press, 1965.

R. Udo. *Geographical regions of Nigeria*. Heinemann, London, 1970.

Journals

African Development (from 1977 called *New African Development*) (London)

Cahiers d'Etudes Africaines (Paris)

Focus (New York)

Geographical Magazine (London)

Geography (Sheffield)

Jeune Afrique (Paris)

Journal of Modern African Studies (Cambridge)

West Africa (London)

INDEX

agriculture, commercial, 3, 20, 21, 22, 23, 24, 27, 28, 29, 30, 36, 42, 68, 75, 77, 108

biomass, 14, 15, 16, 33, 48, 49, 51, 54

capital, 20, 25, 28, 78, 79, 96
cattle, 15, 25, 26, 51, 52, 53, 57, 59, 60, 61, 62, 64, 65, 66, 68, 71, 72, 74, 75, 82, 83, 84, 85, 86, 92, 98, 103, 109, 112, 113; stall feeding, 25, 61, 62, 74, 83, 84, 86
circuits, 18, 52, 53, 54, 72, 73, 110
colonial administration, 3, 28, 29, 38, 45, 46, 75, 103, 107, 110, 114
communications, 3, 20, 27, 28, 42, 89, 99, 100, 103, 105, 106, 107, 115, 118
companies, 28, 42, 43, 96, 107
compounds, 17, 24, 26, 38, 39, 52, 57, 59, 63, 83, 86, 87
conditions, environmental, 1, 3, 5, 10, 11, 15, 16, 18, 20, 21, 22, 23, 43, 46, 52, 56, 64, 66, 69, 72, 74, 81, 83, 85, 88, 93, 94, 95, 118, 119
co-operative societies, 47, 68, 107, 116, 117, 118
crafts, 26, 109, 110
crop associations, 19, 35, 36, 37, 38, 40, 44, 54, 55, 63, 83, 85, 87, 98
crop rotations, 61, 77
crop sequences, 19, 35, 39, 40, 59, 61
crop successions, 20, 55, 85, 87, 98
crops: cash, 20, 21, 27, 29, 36, 37, 38, 45, 46, 58, 63, 64, 65, 66, 75, 76, 77, 78, 79, 85, 86, 96; perennial, 21, 36, 42, 70, 85; staple, 24, 36, 37, 38, 44, 54, 58, 59, 61, 77, 78, 83, 84, 85, 86
cultivable land, 17, 21, 36
cultivation: permanent, 1, 19, 20, 21, 35, 36, 37, 38, 39, 45, 56, 60, 61, 64, 83, 84, 85, 86, 88; rotational fallow, 1, 18, 19, 20, 21, 36, 56, 57, 58, 60, 83, 88; shifting, 1, 16, 17, 18, 19, 20, 21, 23, 56, 58, 117; subsistence, 1, 3, 23, 24, 25, 26, 27, 36, 47, 59, 66, 68, 71, 119

development, 3, 28, 42, 48, 64, 65, 68, 75, 95, 115, 116, 118, 119
diseases, 18, 20, 21, 26, 27, 29, 37, 43, 44, 47, 51, 52, 71, 72, 83, 90, 91, 92, 95, 112
drought, 18, 48, 69, 70, 71, 72

ecosystems, 5, 6, 10, 11, 13, 14, 15, 16, 18, 21, 22, 23, 34, 69, 75, 83
education, 3, 23, 30, 113, 114, 116, 118, 119
emigration, 38, 60
energy, 2, 11, 12, 13, 14, 15, 16, 17, 20, 21, 22, 42, 64, 89, 119; solar, 5, 12, 13, 14, 15, 17, 22, 40, 42
erosion, 33, 40, 41, 59, 61, 62, 64, 85, 86
European involvement, 3, 28, 64, 65, 66, 82, 105, 107, 114
evaporation, 11, 12, 14, 33, 70, 73, 80, 81, 93, 94
evapo-transpiration, 9, 12, 31, 43, 48
exports, 2, 3, 4, 20, 21, 27, 29, 36, 44, 45, 58, 64, 65, 68, 78, 104, 107

fadama land, 63
fallow, 17, 18, 19, 20, 35, 36, 37, 39, 43, 56, 58, 59, 60, 63, 77, 79, 83, 84, 85, 87, 88, 98
family, 22, 23, 24, 25, 26, 28, 38, 42, 43, 52, 55, 57, 60, 63, 117
farming units, 25, 26
fences, 24, 48, 52, 60, 63, 66, 83, 84
fertiliser, 2, 5, 16, 20, 21, 25, 27, 38, 60, 64, 77, 96, 98
fertility, 1, 3, 21, 35, 38, 40, 43, 45, 52, 55, 56, 60, 62, 64, 84, 85, 86, 88
fishing, 60, 64, 89, 93, 94, 96, 97, 98, 109, 117
flooding, 21, 48, 51, 63, 74, 75, 79, 80, 89, 93, 94, 97, 98, 117
fuel, 22, 27, 50, 83, 109, 119

game, 49, 50, 51, 68, 69, 70, 71, 72, 92
gardens, 19, 20, 21, 24, 34, 35, 42, 55, 56, 59, 63, 72, 83, 85, 86, 88
grazing, 3, 6, 15, 18, 25, 48, 49, 51, 52, 53, 54, 59, 60, 61, 62, 63, 71, 72, 73, 74, 83, 85, 89, 92, 94, 99

Hadley cells, 7, 8, 11
herding, 1, 23, 27, 49, 50, 51, 52, 53, 54, 62, 69, 70, 71, 74, 75, 85
herdsmen, 18, 22, 23, 25, 26, 52, 53, 71, 72, 73, 74, 85, 112, 117
home bases, 18, 72, 74
hunting and gathering, 1, 15, 22, 26, 33, 34, 50, 55, 56, 70, 71, 89, 94, 96
hydro-electric power, 85, 88, 117
hydrographic cycle, 12

immigration, 29
implements, 23, 26, 34, 37, 50, 64, 70, 83, 87, 93, 94, 96, 98, 103
imports, 2, 3, 20, 22, 27, 44, 100, 101, 107, 109, 110
insolation, 33, 42
irrigation, 11, 20, 22, 23, 28, 37, 59, 61, 62, 63, 64, 68, 69, 75, 76, 77, 78, 79, 80, 85, 88, 89, 92, 94
inter-tropical convergence zone (ITCZ), inter-tropical front, 7, 8

labour, division of, 24, 26, 39, 55, 71, 96, 98, 110, 111
land: consolidation, 66, 67; tenure, 18, 20, 22, 24, 26, 28, 29, 30, 38, 39, 42, 43, 57, 59, 60, 63, 66, 67, 73, 76, 77, 78, 83, 118; use, 3, 16, 18, 22, 25, 29, 39, 41, 42, 43, 55, 57, 59, 63, 64, 66, 70, 84, 97
laterite (lateritic ironstone), 33, 48, 86, 104
leaching, 14, 33, 40

machinery, 2, 20, 22, 25, 27, 28, 30, 37, 64, 94, 96, 97, 116
mailo land, 29, 30
manufacturing, 3, 5, 22, 27, 42, 46, 75, 96, 101, 106, 107, 109, 110

121

manure, 19, 21, 24, 25, 37, 38, 47, 52, 55, 59, 60, 61, 62, 64, 83, 84, 85, 86, 87, 88
market cycles, 110, 111
market gardening, 29, 66, 78
markets, 21, 29, 30, 42, 45, 58, 66, 71, 77, 94, 100, 107, 108, 109, 110, 111, 112; periodic, 108, 110, 111
marketing, 3, 28, 96
marketing boards, 28, 45, 68, 107
migration, 38, 42, 118

nomadic units, 52, 73
nomads, 18, 22, 23, 52, 53, 62, 72, 73, 74, 78, 80, 83, 85
nutrients, 13, 14, 15, 16, 17, 19, 20, 21, 22, 33, 34, 35, 40, 42, 54, 56, 64, 93, 94

organic matter, 6, 12, 13, 14, 15, 17, 22, 33, 43, 94
output per man hour, 21, 26

pastoralism, 11, 18, 23, 48, 51, 53, 71, 72, 73, 74, 75, 78, 80, 83, 89
pasture, 18, 25, 52, 53, 54, 59, 60, 62, 72, 73, 74, 75, 81, 84, 85, 98
pesticides, 21, 27, 64, 92
pests, 18, 21, 74, 87
photosynthesis, 13, 17, 22, 40, 83
plantations, 22, 23, 28, 35, 45, 46, 47, 65, 83, 84, 85, 97, 113, 118
population, 3, 5, 18, 24, 25, 32, 38, 51, 56, 58, 64, 66, 71, 72, 74, 78, 80, 85, 92, 97, 99, 105, 108, 113, 114, 116, 117, 118, 119; density, 1, 18, 20, 21, 25, 36, 38, 44, 56, 57, 58, 60, 61, 64, 86, 94, 105
predators, 21, 24, 34, 93, 94
prices, 2, 4, 20, 29, 30, 45, 46, 71, 119
primary production, 3, 14, 17, 22, 27, 42, 107
processing of farm produce, 37, 78, 84, 94, 96, 113, 116
profit, 23, 26, 27, 28, 42, 45, 47, 71, 78, 96

railways, 27, 64, 65, 71, 72, 77, 78, 89, 103, 104, 106, 107, 112, 113, 117
rainfall, 1, 6, 7, 8, 9, 10, 11, 12, 13, 14, 15, 31, 33, 37, 40, 42, 43, 48, 49, 50, 51, 54, 55, 58, 64, 66, 68, 69, 70, 71, 72, 73, 74, 76, 81, 82, 85, 93, 98
resettlement, 92, 95, 117, 118
respiration, 13, 42, 83

roads, 3, 28, 29, 42, 53, 56, 72, 78, 83, 86, 89, 100, 101, 103, 104, 105, 109, 112, 114, 116, 117

seasonal occurrences, 1, 6, 9, 10, 11, 14, 26, 28, 38, 42, 45, 48, 50, 51, 54, 55, 60, 70, 71, 73, 75, 80, 81, 89, 91, 93, 109, 112, 118
seasons: dry, 8, 11, 14, 33, 34, 48, 49, 50, 51, 52, 53, 54, 59, 62, 63, 70, 71, 72, 73, 74, 75, 87, 89, 94, 98, 112, 118; wet, 37, 43, 51, 52, 58, 59, 62, 70, 71, 73, 74, 75, 86, 87, 89, 98, 100, 104, 109
settlements, 17, 18, 19, 20, 22, 24, 28, 35, 37, 38, 39, 44, 50, 52, 53, 54, 55, 56, 57, 62, 63, 66, 68, 72, 74, 75, 76, 77, 82, 85, 86, 88, 89, 90, 92, 97, 104, 105, 108, 114, 116, 117, 118
shirika programme, 66, 68
soil, 5, 12, 13, 14, 15, 16, 17, 18, 19, 20, 21, 22, 23, 24, 25, 27, 33, 34, 35, 37, 38, 39, 40, 41, 42, 43, 45, 48, 49, 50, 52, 54, 55, 56, 58, 59, 60, 61, 64, 66, 76, 80, 82, 83, 84, 85, 86, 94, 97, 98, 99; raised beds, 64
soil mounds, 20, 35, 39, 55, 56, 58, 87
soil ridges, 20, 40, 59, 61, 63, 86, 88, 98
storage, 12, 13, 33, 35, 39, 66, 70, 83, 84, 85, 87, 112
systems: agricultural, 1, 3, 5, 16, 17, 18, 20, 21, 22, 23, 24, 29, 56, 57, 64, 78, 83, 88; atmospheric, 7, 8; biological, 5, 94; ecological, 5, 6, 12, 13, 14, 15, 19, 33, 93; economic and social, 3, 5, 28, 72, 112

technology, 3, 18, 20, 21, 22, 25, 26, 37, 40, 61, 64, 86, 87, 94, 96, 98, 100, 103, 113, 119
temperature, 6, 9, 10, 12, 15, 33, 40, 42, 43, 45, 70, 72, 74, 81, 83, 93
terraces, 40, 41, 60, 61, 62, 86, 88
transhumance, 53, 72
transpiration, 12, 14, 33
tsetse flies, 51, 72, 83, 92

ujamaa villages, 118

vegetation, 1, 5, 6, 10, 11, 12, 14, 15, 16, 17, 19, 20, 21, 24, 27, 31, 33, 34, 36, 37, 48, 49, 51, 54, 56, 81, 82, 90, 92, 100; burning, 15, 34, 48, 50, 51, 54, 55, 81; clearing, 15, 20, 21, 26, 33, 34, 35, 36, 37, 39, 40, 48, 50, 51, 54, 55, 56, 58, 72, 81, 82, 85, 97, 98

work, 3, 5, 20, 21, 23, 25, 26, 27, 28, 29, 37, 38, 44, 46, 47, 54, 56, 59, 61, 64, 68, 72, 79, 80, 96, 117, 118, 119

yields, 17, 21, 22, 23, 25, 27, 39, 43, 56, 58, 59, 61, 77, 78, 79, 83, 85, 94

zoning, 1, 6, 11, 14, 27, 29, 48, 56, 57, 66, 81, 82, 84, 90